BITTERSWEET TREASURES
A Father's Journey Through Loss and Healing

By Matt Mauser

with Katie Brandenburger

Bittersweet Treasures:
A Father's Journey Through Loss and Healing
Author: Matt Mauser
Contributing Author: Katie Brandenburger
Editor: Taylor Brien
Contributing Editor: Carla Albano
Contibuting Writer: Dave Wilson
Proofreader: Lyda Rose Hartley
Cover Design: Nicole Wurtele
Interior Layout: Griffin Mill

All images in this book are courtesy of Matt Mauser.

ISBN: 979-8-9913280-2-9

PUBLISHED BY CG SPORTS PUBLISHING

AN IMPRINT OF
NICO 11 PUBLISHING & DESIGN
MUKWONAGO, WISCONSIN
MICHAEL NICLOY, PUBLISHER
www.nico11publishing.com

Quantity order requests can be emailed to:
mike@nico11publishing.com

Printed in The United States of America

TABLE OF CONTENTS

PROLOGUE

"Is Christina OK?" came a panicked voice from the other end of the line.

"Why?" I asked, feeling the beat of my heart pound faster in my chest.

"Because Kobe's dead." The blood drained from my face as the reality of those words set in. The phone dropped from my hand and I fell to my knees, pressing my palms to my forehead and shutting my eyes impossibly tight – as though squeezing them shut might shield me from the most unimaginable news that Kobe Bryant's death signified. If Kobe had died, it meant only one thing: Christina, my wife of 15 years and the mother to our three young children, was also dead.

When a traumatic event happens, you're never prepared for it. No matter what. You can see the drama of a tragedy unfold on television or online, happening to someone else, and say to yourself, *Man, that would never happen to me*, because it's so horrific. Unreal. Unthinkable.

But then it does. Something so gut-wrenching that it literally takes your breath away. It makes you physically ill and emotionally disjointed.

That's what happened to me.

On the morning of January 26, 2020, my wife, Christina, kissed me goodbye then headed to John Wayne Airport in Orange County, California, where she boarded a helicopter bound for a basketball tournament she was coaching in Thousand Oaks, California. On board was L.A. Lakers legend Kobe Bryant, Kobe's daughter,

Gianna, and six others: John, Keri, and Alyssa Altobelli; Payton and Sarah Chester; and pilot Ara Zobayan. The helicopter crashed enroute, leaving no survivors. Life as I knew it, was over.

Living life without her was unfathomable to me. She was my rock. My compass. How was I supposed to navigate through this? Raise three children on my own? Keep it together and provide for my family?

My journey toward healing from such a significant loss has taken me down a long, hard road through some dark places. Many times I've wanted to give up – to stick my head in the sand until it was all over. But I couldn't do that to my kids, and I'm glad I didn't. I chose to keep living, keep moving forward, and above all else... figure out who I was as a parent, without her.

CHAPTER 1:
INTO THE SPOTLIGHT

"Stop, stop, stop!" Simon Cowell shouted in the middle of my performance. "The sound is just awful. It's tinny, it's horrible."

Standing under the searing studio lights on the audition stage for the television show, *America's Got Talent*, I retreated into my head. Somehow I had managed to find myself in front of a panel of judges including Cowell, Heidi Klum, Howie Mandel, and Sofia Vergara; a place I never expected to be. Yet here I was.

I've been a performer for most of my life, so I'm used to being in front of people. I wrote my first song when I was eight, played guitar as a teenager, was an All-American swimmer at Cal Poly-San Luis Obispo; I've been the frontman for a Frank Sinatra tribute big band for more than 10 years; and I've led the largest party band in Southern California for more than two decades. Performing on stage never really freaked me out. But this time it did, because I was singing for my wife, Christina. I was singing for my kids. And I was doing it on national television. I knew that telling the story of our life, and her death, was going to be an emotional roller coaster.

• • • • •

In January of 2021, I was still reeling from Christina's death and the challenges that came with raising three children as a single father during the COVID-19 pandemic. At some point I found my footing and got into a routine with my kids, and life started to slowly pull together. On January 25, 2021, the day before the one-year anniversary of Christina's passing, I decided to perform a virtual benefit concert with the big band for the newly-formed Christina Mauser Foundation, which was established to provide scholarships for female high school senior student-athletes – a cause Christina was passionate about. The concert was a success, attracting thousands of viewers and generous donations. We had a special guest, Frank Stallone (Sylvester Stallone's brother), perform with us, as well as my daughter, Penny. It was a beautiful night and a great way to celebrate Christina's life.

Concert for Christina

Two days later, a talent scout from *America's Got Talent* called. I didn't recognize the number, so I let it go to voicemail and went about my day. When I picked up the message a few hours later, my thoughts began to race. *An audition for reality television?* I'd seen parts of the show before, and knew there were a lot of performers whose stories tugged at the heartstrings of viewers as a way to get ratings. Did I really want to be a part of that?

I was hesitant at first and didn't immediately return his call. I paced back and forth in my living room, thinking about the repercussions of doing such a show, and finally settled down at the brown upright Yamaha piano that had always been a source of solace for me. I closed my eyes and began to play, my fingers moving fluidly across the keys through a song I had written about Christina in the months after her death, and let the feeling of it overtake me. When I opened my eyes at the song's end I knew I had a decision to make, but it wasn't one I was going to make lightly. I had two main concerns: How would this affect my children? How could I do it in a way that honored my wife and didn't make it seem like I was trying to capitalize on her death? A big part of me didn't want the publicity surrounding Christina's death to resurface. It was too painful.

Then something clicked. I started to view it as an opportunity. Not to win, but to be an example of resilience for my kids and to keep their mother's memory alive. It was important to show my children that even if you lose the most important person in your life, you have to continue living. You have to fight the fear, the grief, the hollowness, and the all-consuming sadness to find that glimmer of hope. Of joy. I'm not saying it's easy, because it's not. But you have to try.

I pulled my phone off the top of the piano and dialed Christina's mother, Tita. She is a very loving, family-first woman who lives and breathes for her children and grandchildren, and I value her opinion. "You'd be crazy not to do it," she said.

I thanked her and ended the call, then scrolled through my phone until I reached Christina's brother, Matt. "You should absolutely do it," he told me. "No question."

Even with the support of Christina's family, I found myself doubting the situation. I finally called my manager, John McEntee, and he said, "Performing is what you've done for twenty years. Do you want to keep working, or do you want to keep being depressed?"

As I sat contemplating the pros and cons of what auditioning would mean, something stuck with me. Specifically, "You have to try." So I did.

• • • • •

The audition process happened over the course of two days. Since there was still caution around the pandemic, they announced that there would only be a few staff members in the auditorium during the auditions, not an entire studio audience. The producers put each act up in their own hotel room close to the venue the day before the actual performances in order to film the individual or group's backstory.

When my kids and I first arrived on day one at the Pasadena Civic Auditorium, where they were shooting the show, we were about an hour early. We sat in our SUV and I tried to entertain my 13-year-old daughter, Penny, my 11-year-old son, Tom, and my five-year-old daughter, Ivy, by playing the game 20 Questions. When the time came to go inside, the producers immediately escorted me to an interview room, leaving my children with a member of the *America's Got Talent* staff.

I stepped through the door that led to a small conference room they'd turned into a production set – with dramatic lighting, backdrops, and props – and sat on a couch across from Terry Crews, the host of the show. I began telling our story as best I could, starting with life before Christina, moving through the incredible life I shared with her, and finally onto the shattered existence I was experiencing now that she was gone. While I was going through this deeply poignant interview, my mind drifted back to my kids and the fact that someone I didn't know was caring for them. The producers assured me that they would be fine, but it was hard to have them out of my line of sight in an unfamiliar environment.

However, after only an hour of being watched by the *America's Got Talent* staff, the producers asked if there was anyone else I could call to come help with the children. As it turns out, three kids were a little too much for the staff to handle, in addition to the other acts. I reached out to Christina's mom and her husband who, without hesitation, drove the 45 miles from Huntington Beach to take over. They ended up staying overnight in the same hotel as the kids and me, and spent nearly the entire next day with us as well. I felt indebted to them for being such a huge help, which was a reality check in my role as a single father.

When we went back for the second day, we spent a lot of time waiting in a huge conference room filled with other acts, though everyone was still practicing some form of social distancing. It was organized chaos, and I was trying to stay positive but the kids were bored, even with everyone else rehearsing. Acrobats, singers, dancers, magicians, you name it – they were all around us. I was ushered to another room for meetings with producers and Terry Crews several times. I'd talk with them again and again and it would get really emotional. And then I'd go back to waiting.

Penny, my oldest daughter, vividly recalls that day: "I remember it being nerve-wracking. We were only there to spread our story, not because my dad wanted to go on *America's Got Talent.* He wouldn't just do that out of the blue. I was nervous, not thinking about what the judges would think of my dad, but what the world would think of him. We were going through a lot and COVID was still around, and everyone was separated. For a long time, our family had been isolated and lonely, and this was the first time that we were reintroduced to other people. It was almost surreal. I was trying not to cry, and I was telling my siblings, 'Don't cry, don't cry, *don't cry.'* It was tough. I wanted to look presentable and strong in the public eye. I wanted to show the world that we were strong even though we were struggling."

Finally a producer called out, "All right, Matt, you're up!"

I found the way to my mark and looked around the large, but nearly empty, auditorium, imagining it filled with hundreds of people. My kids were waiting in the wings, and my mind wandered back to my children because being physically away from them was an interesting experience. Even though they were nearby, I could not be there to be Dad. Grandma was there, but it wasn't Dad. I didn't want them to feel abandoned.

Simon's voice snapped me back to the present. "Hello, nice to meet you," he said with a smile.

"It's nice to meet you, too," I replied.

"Use your mic." Howie pointed to the microphone hanging limply by my side in a hand that looked like mine, but felt like someone else's.

Then it clicked. I pulled the mic up to my mouth, "Check one, two. Oh, there it is," I said with a nervous laugh. I was off to a great start.

"OK, what's your name, please?" Simon asked.

"My name is Matt Mauser."

"And where are you from, Matt?"

"I'm from Huntington Beach, California."

"How old are you?"

"I'm fifty-one."

"OK Matt, so why AGT? What are you going to do for us today?"

"I'm a singer, and I'm here because my wife and I were both school teachers. We retired from teaching so that I could do the music full-time, and she got the opportunity to coach girls' basketball with Kobe Bryant. But, on January 26, of 2020 I lost my wife...in the same helicopter crash that killed Kobe Bryant."

As I explained the rest of our story to the judges, all I could think about were my kids and Christina. My stomach was in knots and my head felt fuzzy. I was going through the motions, trying to put myself in the right frame of mind to do Christina justice. To make her proud. It was extremely difficult to get through, but I pushed past the pain of retelling it and ultimately I think it was worth the effort.

I ended with, "It's been a rough year, but here I am."

"Good for you," Simon responded. He asked about my kids, so they stepped within view from the wings to say hello. "OK, well I'm not going to ask anything else, Matt. All I can say is best of luck."

"Against All Odds" by Phil Collins is the song the producers picked for me to sing. I had a fear of singing in front of Simon because of his history of extreme criticism, but this was a song I knew I could do. I didn't have to hit really high notes or do vocal jumping jacks. It was well within my wheelhouse.

So I got ready, steeled myself, and began. About three seconds into it is when I heard Simon shout "Stop, stop, stop! The sound is just awful. It's tinny, it's horrible." For a moment, the hairs on the back of my neck stood up and my stomach churned. But it was fleeting. "I really want to hear this guy sing," Simon told the crew. "Could we please clean it up?"

Terry came over to reassure me. "This is not you, Matt," he said, with compassion in his eyes. "It's technical, and we'll get it fixed soon." Thankfully, Simon hadn't been talking about me. There was something wrong with my microphone.

As they tried to fix the problem, I had a moment of clarity, thanks to Christina. The anxiety started to subside and my nerves were no longer on edge. I just stood there and thought, *You know what? Bring it on*. I wasn't afraid of whatever was coming next because I wasn't there to win. I was there to prove a point...that against all odds everything would be OK.

When the technical issue was resolved and it was time to begin again, I did what I've always done on stage. I started to put on a show. But with each lyric I sang, the strangest feeling came over me. My wife was right there. I felt her presence and was thinking, *Here we are, honey. I'm doing this for you*. I opened up and sang my heart out with pure, raw emotion. I hardly even looked at the judges. I was no longer concerned about them or the show.

I might not have picked it, but as I was singing it, I knew it was telling our story. At the end of the song, I lost my composure. The tears started falling as I sang the last line: "Take a look at me now..." Although "now" was barely audible as I choked up for all the world to see. Closing my eyes, wiping the wetness from my cheeks, I took a step back and tried to collect myself. That's when I heard the cheers. From the wings, from the judges, and from the entire *America's Got Talent* staff. I looked up and saw Simon, Heidi, Sofia, and Howie all standing, hands clapping.

When all of their feedback was taking place, I didn't even process it. All I could think about was Christina. I was talking to her in my head, like, *This is it. Here we are. We did it.* I felt really connected to her at that moment. I knew what the judges were saying but it was almost like I was floating above everything that was happening. It was a very bizarre experience. When you finish what you came to do, and then you get recognition and praise, it's beautiful. But it's also kind of like, *Is this all there is?* I didn't have my partner to share it with. Even though I felt her spirit, I couldn't hold her, laugh with her, hug her, and tell her how much I missed her.

I wanted the world to feel how much I love my wife. And I think that's what came through. She and I had worked so hard to get to this place, this level of performing. She was the brains of our operation, the one running the show behind the scenes, making sure everything went according to plan. But she's not here anymore. She's just...gone.

I've re-watched my audition on YouTube. I know the judges' comments were so positive. Heidi almost started crying: "When you were singing it, it definitely went inside of me. It was beautiful, it was sad, and as a man, as a strong man standing there, I don't know, it was very special."

Howie's words got to me: "We felt your emotion. And regardless of what anybody does on that stage, if you're able to move strangers and we can feel it in our hearts – and I'm not only speaking about everybody at this table, but everybody at home that heard that – I mean, there aren't words to describe it."

Sofia, I think it was heavy for her: "It was very emotional, very touching. Thank you. Thank you for being here."

While I was in the moment, trying to process everything, Simon threw me a curveball. He asked me something I hadn't even considered, "Matt, what would you like to happen if you did well on this show?"

"I would like to um...that's a good question. I haven't gotten that far." There was a brief moment of silence while I tried formulating an answer in my head. "I would like to make sure my children see that in spite of the grief that we've been through this year, that that grief is not going to define who we are as a family," I said. "And that my children see that you have to find joy in life and you have to continue. If this can in any way help my children to chase their dreams, then I'll take it."

One by one, the judges smiled and gave me a "Yes" to go on to the next round. Then Simon spoke again, "You know what, Matt? Of this I am a hundred percent certain. The audience, along with me, want to give you your fourth 'Yes,' Good luck." The kids came out on stage and I picked Ivy up, then embraced them all as the four judges gave another standing ovation. Sharing that moment with my children was indescribable.

After filming in April, my episode aired in July. The response was overwhelming. Once again, we were back in the news. We had interview requests from all over the country. Carson Daly did a short piece on *The Today Show* and there was all this buzz. The audition clip got more than ten million views online. I received thousands of emails and messages of support via social media. It was humbling, but it wasn't why I put myself out there. I did it because it was the next step in the healing process.

America's Got Talent
Audition

Even though all four judges had given me a "Yes" to move on, I had to go up against five other acts in a "Wildcard" runoff for the final spot in the official second round of the competition. Our performances would air exclusively on Peacock during a special show, and the audience would be voting via Twitter.

The producers wanted me to do another sad song, Roberta Flack's "First Time Ever I Saw Your Face." I was going to roll with it, because they thought it would keep me connected to the audience and my story. They paired me with a singing coach, who had a few ideas that I didn't agree with. "Bring your voice out a bit. Try sounding a little more like Ed Sheeran," she said. But that wasn't me.

I didn't want to keep singing sad songs. Getting through the first round of interviews took a lot out of me. I hated rehashing my grief – I couldn't even handle talk therapy. I know it works for a lot of people, but I never felt like repeating all of this helped me move on. I found therapy in making new memories with my kids, getting back in the pool and swimming, performing; doing all the things I loved to do. I'll never forget Christina, but I want to remember how she lived. Not just how she died.

I arrived at the Dolby Theater in Hollywood ready to sing the Roberta Flack song. The more I tried to tell myself I could do it, the more it felt like a lie. Suddenly, I didn't care how they wanted me to perform. I wanted to do a song that represented the real me; one that I loved and would make my wife and kids proud. Roberta Flack is great, but it just wasn't the time nor place for that type of music for me.

"What would you like to perform instead, Matt?" the producers asked. "We're getting down to the wire, so we need you to pick a song."

I didn't hesitate. "'The Way You Look Tonight' by Frank Sinatra." It was the song from the first dance at our wedding, and the last song we danced to in October of 2019. It was perfect.

"Matt, you know our audience. They're not going to get this," they warned me. I didn't heed their advice, and stood my ground. I have a passion for singing Sinatra, and I wanted to do a song that had a heartfelt meaning behind it. If people connected with it, great! If they couldn't because the show appealed to a younger crowd who might not understand how powerful a Sinatra song could be, so be it. It was the right thing for me to do.

I went out there and gave it my all. After three days of voting via Twitter, the results came in. I was the first runner up. I had lost, ending my time on *America's Got Talent*. And I was totally OK with it, knowing it was probably for the best.

Second America's Got Talent *Performance*

CHAPTER 2:
ANOTHER DOOR OPENS

About a month after my exit from *America's Got Talent*, a most remarkable thing happened: I got a call from David Foster.

Over the past 50 years Foster has been a music industry icon. He began his career in the 1960s, and since that time he has gone on to win 16 GRAMMY Awards from 47 nominations, and received three OSCAR® nominations. He has created songs and albums with everyone from Barbra Streisand to Whitney Houston to Michael Jackson to Madonna and Dolly Parton. He helped discover and launch Céline Dion, Josh Groban, and Michael Bublé, and here he was calling *me* because he heard me sing. It blew my mind.

I was in a drive-thru at Starbucks when I got the call, and I'll never forget that moment. My son was trying to order a sugar-loaded, blended something-or-other and I was insisting that he get something a little healthier when my phone rang.

"Matt, David Foster. I want you to come out and sing Sinatra for me." I felt like a teenager getting a call from their high school crush. I tried to play it cool, but my excitement was palpable.

"Let's do it," I managed to get out. "Say when."

And just like that I started traveling the U.S. and Canada, performing with David Foster.

I first met David in person before a show at The Mission Inn in Riverside, California, on November 3, 2021. I was nervous in anticipation of meeting this legendary musician and producer, so I turned my focus to my manager. We were discussing the songs

I was going to sing when the stage curtain pulled back and David stepped through. He strode into the ballroom where we were waiting and immediately introduced himself to me. "Matt, David. Nice to meet you. Ready to get started?"

My first impression of David was that he was a confident man who was straightforward and direct, and knew what he wanted. He had an almost regal air about him – but not in a way that was off-putting. He radiated talent and greatness, and surrounded himself with people of the same variety. And here I was, set to perform with him. I almost felt like a fish out of water. During rehearsal I walked to the side of David's piano, where he asked what I wanted to sing. The client had requested three songs, so I chose "The Way You Look Tonight," by Frank Sinatra, "Feeling Good," by Michael Bublé (which David had actually produced), and another Sinatra great, "My Way." Knowing that my career was on the line, and that this rehearsal could make or break me, I went all out and belted each song like it was my last chance to perform on stage. David was a man of few words that day, and at the end of "My Way," he said simply, "Awesome." My body relaxed and I let out a sigh of relief.

The intimate ballroom was filled to its capacity of about 200 people in no time. The small stage was set up with David's piano, large speakers, and behind them, the instruments to back up The Beach Boys, who were going to close out the concert. David's wife, Katharine McPhee, opened the show, and I was performing in between the two acts. The event was a success.

I was invited to dinner with David and a handful of other people after the show. I sat right next to him, and he asked me about my story. I wanted to tell him everything, but stay humble at the same time. He was very candid, and the conversation flowed easily. He's a down-to-earth guy who is just really good at what he does. At the end of the night, as we were saying our goodbyes, David turned to me and said, "Matt, we'll work together again."

About a week after The Mission Inn show, my manager had arranged for me to attend David's concert at Segerstrom Center for the Arts in Costa Mesa, California, with my daughter, Penny. He told me to wear a coat, which I thought was odd. We had great seats up in the balcony section, and were enjoying the show, when a man with a microphone came up beside me. "Take this," he said.

I looked up at him, confused, then stood when I heard David say from the stage, "Where's Matt Mauser?" I was completely surprised. He looked up at me and said, "Hey Matt, how are you doing? You want to do a little bit of this song…" he started playing the first few notes of "The Way You Look Tonight." I didn't even have time to react or rehearse, he just put me on the spot then and there. So I went with it.

"Absolutely," I said. So, from the stairs of the balcony section at Segerstrom Center for the Arts, I let it flow. Afterwards I was high on the feeling that I had experienced such a joyous moment. Bittersweet, but joyous nonetheless.

Singing with David Foster at Sergerstrom Center for the Arts

A few weeks later, I got another call from David, "Matt, I need you in Palm Desert." Then, a few weeks after that it was, "Matt, can you make it out to Las Vegas?" That was a big one. Christina and I had always talked about having a residency at the Wynn Hotel in Las Vegas doing my Sinatra show, so this was a dream-come-true moment. On the four-hour drive to Las Vegas, I had a lot of time to reflect and reminisce, remembering the moments with Christina when we discussed what it would be like if we actually made it to Vegas to perform. Would we move the whole family out there? Did they have a good school system for the kids? We were way ahead of ourselves, but it was so good to just sit there and dream with her. She believed in me so wholly and deeply that she pressed me to keep performing any gigs I could that would prepare me for the bright future she saw in store for us. While we were dating, she once told me that she didn't want to live a dull life, and she knew that with me life would never be boring. She saw my sky-is-the-limit attitude and loved the fact that there was always something new.

I arrived at the Wynn and met up with my mom, my aunt, one of my best friends, and my manager. We made our way into the Encore Theater and found our seats, just left of center stage, fifteen rows back. About a half hour into the show, David called out to me from behind his piano, and I made my way down the aisles and up onto the stage. He stood and walked over to me, introducing me to the crowd.

"Matt was on *America's Got Talent*, and he found his niche singing sort of late in life," he said. "He was a school teacher, but he's been singing all over the country. He's worked with me many times on stage." He turned to me as I approached him and said, "Hey Matt, welcome, man," and shook my hand. "Well, you have a unique story. Do you mind sharing with the folks your story?"

"Not at all," I replied. "On January 26 of 2020, I lost my wife in the helicopter crash that killed Kobe Bryant. She was his assistant coach." I could hear the murmurs rush through the crowd as they took in my words. "But tonight is not a night of mourning, it's a night of celebration. This was the dream for my wife and I – to be performing in Vegas." I turned to David. "And to do it with you… this is the first time I've ever performed in Vegas."

David put his hand on my shoulder and said, "I'll tell you this: it's easy to say this will not be the last time you'll perform in Vegas. And I mean it, you're just so incredible and you have such a gift." He looked at the audience with a smile on his face and said, "Wait until you see what this guy can do." I was floored.

"This song, to me, captures Vegas at the highlight of 1966 with Sinatra at The Sands Hotel," I said. The lights dimmed and the large jumbo screen above the stage displayed a Vegas-themed montage of images as I began to sing, "Luck Be a Lady."

I felt the energy of the crowd surge through me, and the spirit of Christina watching over me. Even though I often sing Sinatra, I don't always mimic his stage presence. I put my own twist on each performance. I don't just get up and sing – I perform, and this night was no different. As soon as the horns hit at "Luck be a lady tonight," my hips were swinging, toes were tapping, and arms were waving around in deliberate movements to get the audience up and dancing along with me. It was impossibly perfect, but for one thing: Christina wasn't physically there.

Prior to rehearsal of my next performance with David at the Beverly Hilton Hotel in Beverly Hills, California, he pulled me aside. He looked somewhat serious, yet contemplative, like he didn't know how to tell me what he was going to say. With sincerity in his voice he said, "Matt, can I give you a piece of advice?"

"Of course, anything," I replied, eager to hear his words of wisdom.

"OK, please don't take this the wrong way, but…maybe do a little less dancing," he cautioned. "I don't want it to detract from your voice."

Dancing has been a huge part of my shows, no matter the venue or circumstance. With my rock band, Tijuana Dogs, I'm known for my on-stage antics and really getting the crowd worked up by dancing in the stands and moving around the stage. It is a part of my identity as a performer, and has always come naturally to me. But this was *David Foster* talking. In the music business, David is as good as it gets. When David Foster offers even a crumb of information about what it takes to make it in the music industry, you take note. So I swallowed my pride, shut my mouth, and listened. Humility is important in any industry, but this one especially. You're always working for somebody. You can either be right, or you can work. There are times when you have to just do your job in exactly the manner in which it has been explained to you, and there are other moments when you're given the creative freedom to do your own thing. That is part of what has kept me working for so long. You have to take criticism, and be humble. You also have to know your audience.

So now, when David needs a Sinatra guy, I'm the one he calls. Auditioning for *America's Got Talent* ended up being a blessing. I love performing with him. He has put me in touch with a lot of industry professionals, and allows me to continue telling the story of my wife's life on my terms – in a way that doesn't hurt. David has opened doors for me that I never even knew existed. He has given me the opportunity to find glimmers of hope, rather than focusing on sadness.

One thing I've realized in traveling with the bands and with David, is that I really would give it all up if it meant being with Christina again. The woman who would pass out flyers on the beach to promote my shows, who retired from teaching with me so we could focus on music – the one who helped me grow it into a full-time business? She's not here to experience all of these life-changing events. To watch our kids grow up. She was there for the building of it, but she is not here for the unveiling.

This is the reality of every experience. I spend the majority of my life at odds with my new "normal." Everything that brings joy and happiness is peppered with so much anguish because the love of my life, the mother of my children, isn't here to share it with.

When Christina was here I focused on family, but I also had this intense drive to pursue my passion of creating and performing music – and she supported that. But in raising three kids as a single father, I see that having a career I love and can be proud of is so important, but my kids will always come first. I want to give my children everything I never had as a child, and so much more.

CHAPTER 3:
FINDING NEW HEROES

A hero is typically seen as a mythological figure, often divine or noble, possessing great strength and extraordinary abilities. It also refers to someone admired for their achievements and virtuous qualities. For most young boys, their dad is their hero. But when my dad disappeared from my life at a young age, I had to find new heroes. This chapter is dedicated to all the heroes I found along the way.

Before I ever found myself on a stage, I was a kid navigating the sun-soaked streets of Huntington Beach, California, in search of some semblance of stability.

My parents divorced in 1979, when I was nine years old, and my dad, George, moved to a houseboat 40 miles away in Los Angeles Harbor. He worked odd jobs and came in and out of our lives sporadically, never giving my two younger brothers and I the chance to truly experience what it was like to have a father. I loved my dad and couldn't understand why he would disappear for months and years at a time. I learned early on that if I wanted male role models in my life, it was up to me to go out and find them.

My brothers and I were raised by our mom, Sonja, in an apartment located in the lower-income area of town known as the "Slater Slums."

It was a culturally diverse neighborhood, and most of the kids I grew up with spoke Spanish or Vietnamese as their first language. I picked up a little bit of Vietnamese, but found myself conversationally fluent in Spanish after a year or two. The area was known for crime and break-ins, but I never experienced true fear until our house was burglarized in the middle of the night while we were home. They didn't rob us at gunpoint, but knowing someone could come in and out of our house at any time was unsettling. It happened three times over the course of a couple of years, and I had trouble sleeping because of it until my mid-20s.

Mom worked as a substitute teacher for the Westminster school district, where she eventually got a full-time position. She attended night school two or three days a week to obtain her teaching credential and masters degree, which I always respected, but my brothers and I were home alone a lot. After school we'd drop off our backpacks at the apartment, then run outside to meet up with the neighborhood kids. Our afternoons and evenings were filled with boxing, hide-and-seek, baseball, kickball, building forts, riding our bikes, and playing in the streets well after the streetlights came on. In a way we were raising ourselves. I'd make breakfast every morning and take on some of the cooking duties in the evenings. As the oldest, I felt somewhat responsible for the well-being of my brothers. In a sense, I took on the role of the central male figure of the family, but I was still a child myself and needed guidance.

During summertime, my mom forced me to participate in the Huntington Beach junior lifeguard program. The first year she made me do it, I fought her tooth and nail. I wanted to play baseball all summer, not hang out at the beach. However, it was there I learned respect, teamwork, and water safety. It was through this program that I developed a strong sense of self-worth and discipline. I also learned more about independence because I rode the bus by myself every day to get there. It was an experience that would greatly benefit me later on in life.

Though my relationship with my father was almost nonexistent throughout my youth, over the last several years he and I have formed a strong connection. About being a father, my dad says: "When I had Matt, my first son, it was challenging for me because I never saw myself as a father. I thought, *Holy shit, man, I am a father now. What do I do?* I grew up with dysfunction within my family, and I did not have a good relationship with my own dad. Thus, I did not embrace the idea of fatherhood. It was a huge reality check. The marriage to his mother did not last long, and it was devastating to me. So, I moved out and the children remained with their mother. I stayed away for quite a while. I would visit them infrequently. The reality is that I left Matt at an early age, and he had to find new heroes."

At 10 years old I signed up to be on a baseball team in Huntington Beach's Ocean View Little League. I had a big, boisterous coach named John Beaubien, who took me under his wing. He became like a father to me, giving me tough love when I needed it, and a soft place to land when I needed that, too. He'd spend countless hours helping me hone my skills as a baseball player. He always offered sound advice to my fellow teammates and I about life and baseball, and was quick to remind us that he would put his shoe "up your ass" if you were disrespectful or talked back. I was with Coach Beaubien for three years, from ages 10 to 12, which are easily some of the most formative years in anyone's life. He was supportive in a way I had never experienced before, and helped give me the confidence I needed to become a competitive athlete.

Under the guidance of Coach Beaubien, I developed a deep appreciation for the sport. Standing on the pitcher's mound, throwing pitch after pitch as the opposing team went through their lineup, I felt a sense of confidence. The cheers from the stands, the camaraderie between my teammates, and the rush of running the bases – I couldn't get enough of it. I worked out the kinks in my swing, and led the league with the highest batting average.

On Opening Day in 1981, I was the starting pitcher. Proud of this accomplishment, I knew I had an important job to do. I wanted to help my team and show them they made the right decision by putting me in. After about the second or third inning, I noticed my father had arrived with his new spouse in tow – she was holding my little brother, who was a baby at the time. My brothers and I were scheduled to spend the weekend with my dad following the game. My mother, who was there to support me as well, was unaware of the recent nuptials of her former husband. I watched helplessly from the field as they proceeded to get into a heated argument, yelling so loudly that people were staring. I watched in horror as my mother lunged at my dad's wife screaming, "GIVE ME BACK MY BABY!" Coach Beaubien called time out and walked up to the mound where I stood. I was mortified by the situation, but Coach was unaffected and steely with his resolve. In a calm voice, never looking toward the bleachers and focusing completely on me, he said, "It's not on you. Someday you will grow up to be a man and you'll be able to let go of them and make your own decisions. For now, focus on what's important, Matt, and not what's happening in the stands."

By the time the game ended and the argument had ceased, my mother had left with my brothers, and my father came to give me a hug and asked if I was OK.

"I'm fine," I answered.

"I love you," he replied. He turned to leave, and I could see he was visibly upset. He disappeared from my life for another two years.

I didn't know it at the time, but character-building opportunities such as this one were preparing me to be a supportive and loving dad myself. I saw what I didn't want, and vowed that my kids would never be without their father, so long as there was a breath in me. When Christina died, Coach Beaubien's advice played like a loop in my head, "Focus on what's important, Matt, not what's happening in the stands."

Sports were a haven for me, and they also kept me out of trouble. My natural abilities coupled with my passion for training took my talent to a whole new level. Athleticism runs in my family, so we were always pretty successful and excelled in sports. My father was an athlete. Sinewy and long, he played football, had fast-twitch muscles, and was an avid body surfer at the notoriously dangerous spot in Newport Beach, California, called "The Wedge." His twin sister, Carol, was a champion swimmer and Masters Swimming World Record holder. Though not related by blood, my Uncle Bill, Carol's husband, was a collegiate swimmer and Olympic kayaker who eventually became the swim coach at Newport Harbor High School.

Bill and Carol exposed me to water sports at an early age. I was never in it, per se, but I was always around it when I'd spend time with my cousins, aunt, and uncle. I'd go to swim meets and visit the beach with them during the summer. In some ways, they were gently guiding me toward the sports of water polo and swimming. I call this my "proxy background" in aquatics. Bill and Carol's obvious love of the water was imparted upon me. I would watch the swimmers at the high school and see them in such great shape. They were just a few years older than me and seemed happy, healthy, and ready to take on the world. By introducing me to the water, Carol and Bill would prove to be an essential part of the healing process I would have to go through after losing my wife.

Around the same time sports were woven into my life, music became a part of it, too. My father's side of the family was musically talented. Two of my four aunts were concert pianists, my great-grandmother performed for President Theodore Roosevelt in the White House, and my father played guitar.

I grew up listening to classical music, and was introduced to rock and roll by my 17-year-old Uncle Shane when I was seven. I worked at the Orange County Swap Meet next to Angel Stadium, where Major League Baseball's Angels played, selling speakers with him. We'd spin records like Led Zeppelin, The Rolling Stones, The Beatles, Queen, and Aerosmith while trying to make a sale. I listened intently and learned the lyrics to all those classic rock songs, which would prove useful in my later years as a performer.

When I was eight years old, my mother purchased a guitar for my brother, Gabe. Gabe took lessons, and he'd come home and show me what he'd been taught. I took to it immediately, learning everything I could about how to play. I would steal the sheet music and chord charts to practice. I wrote my first song soon thereafter, called "Cut It Out":

Cut it out, oh baby, cut it out
Quit your foolin' around and get out of town
Cut it out, get off my back
Get on the train track and give me back my Cadillac
Cut it out, Cut it out…

It wasn't much, but when I sang my new song, it was well received. I practiced playing and singing every day. I knew I had a good voice and a strong ear, but music was mesmerizing to me and I was driven to learn more. It almost became an obsession. I would immerse myself in it and spend time learning songs for hours on end and study entertainers like Freddie Mercury, Jim Morrision, Michael Jackson, Prince, and Frank Sinatra, who became my musical heroes and influences. I was fascinated at a young age, which sent me down a path of discovery where I honed and continued to create my own style as a musician and entertainer.

My maternal grandfather, Pat Hawley, was also a father figure during my early years. He was quite the character. Initially from Rhode Island, my grandfather lived in New Jersey for many years, where he was stationed in the military nearby. In 1955, he packed up the family car and drove his wife and three kids across the country to start a new life in Southern California. He opened a used car lot called Hawkeye Motors in Anaheim – about a mile from Disneyland. The business did not go as planned, but Grandpa always had ambition, so he decided he was going to be an actor.

After finding initial dead ends in the entertainment industry, one day my grandfather got a tip about where Frank Sinatra was going to be having lunch. It was at the famous Knickerbocker Hotel in Hollywood, California. Not the shy type, my grandfather approached Sinatra and said, "Hey, Frank, give me a job. They won't give me my Screen Actors Guild card."

He hoped their shared New Jersey roots would endear him to Sinatra. It worked.

Frank said, "Come back here tomorrow and I'll take care of you."

True to his word, Frank Sinatra cast my grandfather in one of his specials sponsored by Chesterfield cigarettes. In it, Sinatra is singing "One for My Baby (And One More For The Road)" to my grandfather, who is acting as a bartender.

*One For My Baby
(And One More For
The Road)*

My grandfather eventually obtained his Screen Actors Guild (SAG) card. He had a long and satisfying character acting career, until a stroke at 58 left him disabled for the remainder of his life. He always credited Frank Sinatra with his success as an actor.

My entire family loved Frank Sinatra for his support of my grandfather, and his voice was a constant in our house. When I was young, my mother would encourage me to sing his songs. As I reflect on it now, the influence of Sinatra upon my life has been a true treasure.

I continued experimenting with music throughout middle school, but when I began high school in 1984 at Edison in Huntington Beach, I wanted to continue playing baseball. On the first day of tryouts, I dressed out and took the field. I was excited to be playing again, and saw a few familiar faces. I also saw that all the kids were much bigger than me, and it was a little intimidating. However, I made the team and continued to play the sport I loved despite my shortcomings.

In physical education class my freshman year, the teacher put all the students at one end of the pool and told us we were going to race. Before I knew it the teacher yelled, "On your mark, get set, GO!" and everyone made a beeline for the other end of the pool. I put my head down, pushed off the side of the pool and swam as fast as I could. I won. The water polo coach had been watching from the stands, scouting for strong swimmers. He approached me after I got out of the water.

"You're a good swimmer," he said. "Why don't you think about coming out for water polo?"

When it was time for water polo tryouts later that afternoon, I realized right away that all those years of baseball and spending time with my Aunt Carol and Uncle Bill may have prepared me for water polo. I was a decent swimmer, though not as fast as the other water polo kids, but I had more hand/eye coordination than the rest of the team. I could tread water in the middle of the pool and shoot the ball from half court. After making the cut, I was either on the field or in the pool every day.

While I loved playing baseball, I was more at home in the water. One day my water polo coach, Matt Whitmore, said to me, "Matt, you've got to really think about swimming. Unless you are going to go pro or play college baseball, you might have a brighter future in the pool. You are a really good swimmer. I think it could get you a job as a lifeguard, and it might even get you a scholarship to college."

That conversation changed the trajectory of my life. I quit baseball my senior year of high school and focused on swimming and water polo. I grew from 5'9" to 6'1" and watched my times get faster and faster due to my additional strength, height, and length. I broke the school record in the 100-yard backstroke that same year.

I remember sitting in economics class the day after that swim meet when the morning announcements came on over the PA system. They said, "Congratulations to Matt Mauser for breaking the school record in the 100-yard backstroke."

Everybody in the class turned to me, surprised. I got high-fives and pats on the back, and the teacher made the whole class applaud. I sat there and thought, *Is this something I can do*?

Being in the water gave me a peaceful reprieve from everyday life. I was purely focused on what was happening in real time. It became therapy for me and a way to shut everything out. Stroke after stroke I stared at that black line on the bottom of the pool, which eradicated any self-doubt or worries that took up space in my head. With that, I became an even more confident swimmer.

I got recruited to play water polo at Golden West College, a junior college in Huntington Beach, and from there I received some financial help to swim at Cal Poly-San Luis Obispo where I became the top backstroker.

I grew to 6'2" in my sophomore year of college, which helped my times improve even more. In a dual meet against University of California-Davis I made my NCAA cut times midseason. I clocked a 1:54.1 time in the 200-yard backstroke, and a teammate of mine turned to me and said, "Holy shit, you're fast."

Throughout my college career, I made two National Collegiate Athletic Association (NCAA) championships and was an All-American in the backstroke, which exposed how much I loved competition.

My high school coach was spot-on when he encouraged me to focus on the pool rather than trying to juggle multiple sports. Swimming taught me discipline and gave me structure. Just as Coach Whitmore had said, it also helped me get a job as a Huntington Beach lifeguard – a dream come true.

I had an unusual path to becoming a lifeguard. Before my senior year in high school, I was in search of a summer job. The City of Huntington Beach had an open janitorial position at Lifeguard Headquarters, and I jumped at the opportunity. While toilets, mops, showers, and sinks became my specialty, I was exceedingly proud to be a member of the lifeguard family. It introduced me to many positive male influences, and gave me a greater purpose. After a full year working on the maintenance crew, one of the chief lifeguards asked if I wanted to transition to becoming a lifeguard.

"Want to trade in your mop for a buoy?" he'd asked. I put the mop back in the bucket and never looked back.

From a distance, my father noticed a profound change in me. Of this time in my life, he recalls: "I was not a good role model for him. Matt had to find some new heroes. He found that in swimming and lifeguarding. One time Matt and I were at Lake Tahoe, and somebody was out in the water drowning. I watched Matt jump in the water to rescue the swimmer, right in front of me. This memory makes me emotional to this day; there is my son, saving somebody's life. He brought the swimmer up to the beach and performed CPR. I sat there and thought, *Oh my God, this is my son. And he is saving lives.* That flipped something inside and Matt became the hero in my life. As his father I was not the hero, but Matt was, and now, still is my hero."

I started to find my way and developed a healthy balance between school, swimming, and lifeguarding during summer breaks. I had a pretty active social life, and hung out with a lot of the football players. One Saturday night a buddy of mine from the football team invited me to a big house party and told me to bring my guitar. At some point during the night, he asked me to play a few songs. Someone turned the stereo down and all eyes were drawn to me.

I started singing "All Shook Up" by Elvis Presley. I really got into it, doing my best Elvis impersonation, and the room erupted in cheers. By the end of the evening I had everyone singing and dancing along with me. People I didn't know were coming up to me, requesting songs, telling me how good I was, and I felt a rush of excitement from all the attention. That was it for me. I had found my calling.

The heroes who guided me along the way never knew their impact, but through them I learned confidence and the willingness to take chances. I was now ready and eager to become an adult.

CHAPTER 4:
ADULTING

I graduated college in 1995 with a degree in Recreation Administration. I became a substitute teacher, which allowed me to continue my career as a lifeguard on the weekends and during the summer. I continued to stay in shape, and played music as often as possible. I didn't know how I was going to do it, but I was determined to make music my career.

Right out of college I met a young woman, and we got married. My jobs as a lifeguard and substitute teacher were going well, but my desire to be a performer became almost an obsession. In the summer of 1997 I took out an ad in the local newspaper and found a bass player. One of my lifeguard friends introduced me to a drummer, and I played guitar and took on lead vocals. We rehearsed in my mom's garage, and were soon performing Johnny Cash, Elvis, and Beatles covers at small clubs across town. A few shows in, I noticed we weren't getting much traction; we needed to shake things up.

I had taken a studio guitar class in 1996 at a local community college to fine tune my guitar skills, and became fast friends with my professor, Dave Murdy. He was only a few years older than me, and had a great sense of humor and undeniable talent as a guitar player. I was drawn to his passion for creating music. When I decided to get serious about the band, I called Dave.

Around this time I had gone on a surfing trip to Mexico where I saw stray dogs roaming the streets in Tijuana. I thought, *Tijuana Dogs, what a cool name for a band.* And that was that. Our band became the Tijuana Dogs, but it was pretty funny in the early days of performing, when people often thought we were a mariachi band. I passed out flyers on the beach for all of our shows, and after a few successful gigs we developed a decent following. We quickly shed the mariachi band label and grew into one of the biggest rock bands in Orange County. We put on a great show. We were silly and fun, and people loved it. I was hooked. I was going to do whatever it took to continue to grow the band.

My wife at the time, however, had a different point of view. One day she confronted me and said, "This wasn't what I signed up for. When we met, you were a substitute teacher and a lifeguard. I wasn't expecting you to have shows every weekend and I don't want this kind of lifestyle." She gave me an ultimatum: "It's either me or the music." It was one of the first times in my life I had total clarity on what I wanted. When she gave me the ultimatum, I knew that someone who would force me to give up something I was so passionate about wasn't meant for me. Six months after that conversation, I was back on the market.

I moved back in with my mom after the divorce, and started saving money to buy a house of my own. I was thriving, and all my worlds were colliding: teacher by day, singer in a popular band at night, and lifeguard on the weekends and during the summer. Everything was rolling along, and I was a swingin' bachelor making money. I had no overhead. I was putting away $50,000-$60,000 a year. I spent next to nothing. Vacations were always taken up by the band. My social life was the band. It was all work and I loved it.

What I didn't love were the hangovers. Being in a band comes with certain stereotypes, and I'm sure I fit the mold in more than one category. Sometimes we'd have shows on a Sunday night and I'd be drinking, singing, and having the time of my life, then have to wake up early the next morning to teach. I'd rally and put on my best face for school, but I wasn't fooling anyone. A few of the other teachers knew I came in hungover a few days, and heard my wild stories of weekend gigs where the crowd would just go nuts. My ostentatious way of living rubbed some people the wrong way, but I was just trying to live my best life. I let myself go every once in a while, but I was keeping it together for the most part.

I bought a house in Huntington Beach in 2001, and a few of my lifeguard buddies moved in with me to help offset the cost of the mortgage. It was a beautiful single story home on a cul-de-sac that we turned into a complete bachelor pad.

A teacher friend, who was a little bit older and wiser than me, once said, "Mauser, some day a girl is going to walk into one of your shows and your life is going to change."

"Hell no," I'd told him. "I've been married, and there's no way I'm going back to that." And I meant it.

But…he was right.

CHAPTER 5:
MATTERS OF THE HEART

By 2003 I was living my own version of a rock-star life as the popularity of the Tijuana Dogs grew. I was still teaching during the day and lifeguarding on the weekends and during summer. It was a crazy time and I thought the single life suited me. I dated, but never wanted anything serious.

My father had the same bachelor mindset, and we shared a similar problem with commitment: "Women were attracted to me, but I had a hard time settling down," my father reflects. "When Matt started performing live, I was proud and shocked because I was not a performer in that style. I too had worked in Hollywood, with movie stars such as John Wayne and Barbra Streisand in the old days, and I see what performers do. When Matt got up and sang, he connected with the people in his audience. And that is what I saw. His magic was his connection. I witnessed Matt's magic over and over. I thought, *What's happening here? It is not just the singing talent.* There is something about his personality that lures people in, especially women. And women threw themselves at him."

One night during the summer of 2003, Tijuana Dogs were playing at a bar in Anaheim. After our show, I was manning the merchandise table, and a woman walked up to me, asking to buy a t-shirt and a CD. I had noticed her singing, dancing, and goofing around during the show. She was with a group of friends, but I remember looking at her thinking, *My God, what a beautiful woman.*

She smiled at me and said, "I'm Christina."

"I'm Matt," I replied.

"You guys are really good. Thanks for the fun!" She took her t-shirt and CD and was gone.

In the following weeks and months, I started to notice Christina in the audience at our shows. One time she came out to a bar called The Harp in Costa Mesa, California. The place was packed, and we were feeding off the crowd's energy. There was a music break during one of the songs, so I walked over and asked her to dance.

"I can't, I have a boyfriend," she said.

"Come on, don't make me look bad," I said in a playful tone.

She was with a friend, who nudged her and yelled, "Go for it!"

Christina relented and danced with me.

Afterward, we walked outside and talked about our backgrounds. We discovered each of us had attended Edison High School in Huntington Beach. I said, "Well, hey, if things don't work out with your boyfriend, come on back."

A few months later, I was performing at a bar in downtown Huntington Beach called Hurricanes. Christina came walking in and it was like reliving the movie *Fast Times at Ridgemont High*. Christina looks *a lot* like the actress Phoebe Cates but even sexier, in my opinion. Christina was a goddess. She approached me in slow motion. It had been a while since I'd last seen her, and I didn't immediately recognize that we had met before. She asked me if I was going to play one of my original songs.

"How do you know that song?" I asked, still oblivious to the fact that we'd already met.

"I have your CD. I have a t-shirt," she said. "Remember me?"

"Not really," I replied, trying to place her.

Then it hit me like a slap to the face. "Oh, yeah, I remember you! You went to Edison, too. How have you been? Good to see you again."

It was July 11, 2004, and Christina was wearing a green top with khaki shorts and flip-flops. She had an incredible figure and gorgeous dark eyes. She was tall, about 5'9", and very athletic-looking. She had swarthy dark skin and a beautiful smile. I couldn't take my eyes off her the rest of the night.

Christina was with a group of friends, and they were having a fun time. By the end of the show I felt compelled to give her my phone number. "If your friends call it a night, you have my number," I told her. She grinned at me as she walked away, arm in arm with her friends.

I had just returned home and was unloading my gear when my phone rang. I answered and Christina said, "Hey, it's me. Come get me."

When I went to pick her up at her friend's house, she was waiting outside as I pulled into the driveway. She hopped in, flashed a brilliant smile and we drove around town, talking and getting to know each other. In true California style, we went to the popular fast food restaurant, Del Taco. Christina was intriguing if not intoxicating, but I didn't really know what to think of her. I wasn't looking to settle down.

Like a gentleman, I returned her to her friend's house, where we sat outside in the car until the early hours of the morning. I had my guitar, so I played some songs for her that I was developing. Christina was so excited and enthusiastic about everything we talked about. She thought I was talented and wanted to know more about my influences.

One of my favorite influences was Hall & Oates. They played

a baseline to the song called "I Can't Go for That" which was the inspiration for "Billie Jean" by Michael Jackson. I remember dancing and goofing around in the car. Christina was laughing, an uncontrollable, infectious laugh. She had the most pure, honest, sincere laugh I had ever heard. I could feel her joy. Everything came so easily between us.

While I did not realize it at the time, and as I reflect upon it now, that moment was when I began to fall in love with her.

I dropped Christina off, then spoke with her every day until she died.

• • • • •

A few weeks into our relationship, I was becoming increasingly nervous. Within two or three months we were profoundly serious. My commitment issues started bubbling to the surface, and I tried to pump the brakes to slow things down. I was falling hard for her and, though my instincts were telling me to stay, my head was telling me it was too much.

We had just finished dinner at my house one evening when I turned to Christina and – against my better judgment – suggested that we take a break. Christina was devastated. Her eyes welled up and she started sobbing. I looked at her and my heart broke. I have never seen anyone have so much grief over a breakup and it crushed me. I couldn't stand seeing her that way.

I said, "OK, OK, OK, do not cry. We will figure it out. Just do not cry." It was at that moment when I realized she was all in, and I knew it was up to me to figure myself out. Christina wanted me and made it quite clear. I had never experienced that before. All. In.

• • • • •

In my life before meeting Christina, I had been winging it. Everything I did was on the fly. Early into our relationship I realized how much of an impact she was having upon me. I was highly unorganized and easily distracted. Christina was unbelievably focused. She set her energy upon straightening up my business with the band.

She looked at me one day and said, "I'm going to get you squared away."

It started with, "You need to buy a computer." So I bought a computer.

"You can't be mailing invoices." We started invoicing online.

"You need a printer." I got a printer.

Christina took over. I began to understand I was not able to do what she did. She was so much smarter than I was. Christina managed the band, managed all the contracts, dealt with the clients, and juggled the travel details. She was everything.

It was unclear what kind of person I needed to be with until I met Christina. Hell, I thought I'd be a perpetual bachelor the rest of my life, so I wasn't even thinking about the type of person I needed until she was right in front of me. I recognized it in Christina. She did not take any crap. She would never be a pushover. Christina could fight for herself, and she could fend for herself. When Christina didn't agree with you or felt like you weren't toeing the line, she had a really strong moral compass, and she was not afraid to confront you. Christina challenged me on everything, which could anger me, but I learned her boundaries.

Penny, our oldest daughter, has a favorite story Christina told her about collaborating with me and the band: "Mom told me this story when Dad couldn't get the mixer board to work for his speakers. 'He was so flustered,' she said, saying 'Christina, I can't get it to come on.' I just remember her laughing and telling me the story as she was putting me down to bed. 'He was so upset,' she told me. 'I asked him, did you turn *on* the panel? And he said, Oh.' He followed it up with, 'I love you. Christina.' Mom could humble Dad so quickly."

Christina was eternally humble. For quite some time while we were dating I had no idea she was an athlete, so I didn't realize what I was up against. One day I was bragging about being a good athlete – especially my basketball skills, which I had picked up during college.

She said, "OK, show me."

We went to the hoops in my front yard and she threw me the ball. I smiled and started dribbling slowly, then made a quick move toward the basket. Before I knew it she was all over me. With her hands in the air and in my face, she was blocking all my shots. She knocked the ball out of my hands and took it straight in for a layup. I could not believe just how incredible she was. She could post up, she could pivot, she could shoot from anywhere. She was unbelievably strong, light on her feet, and moved with finesse. She didn't take it easy on me. On the court, Christina was intimidating.

A few weeks later Christina's younger brother, Jason Morash, was wrestling at Edison, our alma mater. Christina had to go pick him up, and she asked if I would go with her. As we walked into the school, I tried to play it cool and said, "Hey, let me show you something." I took her to the Hall of Fame where the best athletes for each individual sport are recognized.

"Check this out," I said, pointing to my name for the backstroke record.

She said, "Oh wow, congratulations!"

"Yeah, pretty cool, huh?" I replied, quite proud of myself.

Christina smiled and made her way down the wall of names. "Here's me here…here…and here," she said, pointing to her plaques. Her name was on the Hall of Fame wall three times, once as Athlete of the Year, and twice for her junior and senior year in basketball. Christina was elite.

Dave White, her high school coach, is a legendary Southern California basketball and CIF Championship football coach. He said she was one of the most intelligent players he had ever coached. She was intense, she was a floor general, she did not let anybody slack. Christina, while in her opponent's face, could also be disarming with her sense of humor or her nurturing reassurance. Christina had all these elements within her that very few people possess. Great athletes are more intelligent than anything else.

Christina's intelligence and intensity are what set her apart, and what made her so fierce. We went to watch her cousin play in a basketball game, and as a spectator Christina was super intense, screaming, "Hey, pick it up! Get in there!"

I was taken aback. She was not like any girl I'd ever dated before. I didn't know what to make of her. The entire game I sat, observing her, all the while thinking to myself, *Is this the type of girl I want in my life?* By the time the game was over I realized with absolute certainty that she wasn't just the *type* of girl I wanted in my life, she was *exactly* the girl I wanted in my life.

One afternoon my mom and I were having lunch and Christina joined us. At the end of our lunch, Christina stepped out to use the restroom and Mom turned to me and said, "You're thirty-four years old. That is the most beautiful woman I've ever seen you with, in every way. If you let her go, you are a fool." I knew she was right.

That day I took Christina to South Coast Plaza, a mall in Costa Mesa. We were window shopping and walked by the jewelry store chain, Zales. I pulled her inside the store, and playfully said, "Pick one."

"Are you serious?" she asked.

"Yes, I think we should get married," I said with a dopey grin on my face.

She arched an eyebrow and looked me square in the eye. "Are you asking me to marry you?"

"Yes," I replied.

She gave me a wicked grin. "I will marry you. But I do not want to get a ring at Zales."

That exchange was a shining example of our dynamic. She had an enthusiastic sense of timing and humor. Afterward, it began to rain, but despite the weather we decided to go to the Happiest

Place on Earth, The Disneyland Resort. I know few people who go to Disneyland/Disney's California Adventure in the rain, but for us it was the perfect ending to a perfect day, and the launch of our future together. I remember standing in line at the Tower of Terror – the ride seemed metaphorically very appropriate. I was an engaged man, ready to take the ride of my life. It was terrifying and exhilarating all at once.

Christina ended up picking an engagement ring from Ballard & Ballard, a 100-year-old jeweler in Huntington Beach. She wasn't pretentious, but she had good taste.

"I want one that's quality and says you love me," she told me. I would have spent every penny I had on the perfect token of my love for her, but she wasn't like that. It was one of the many reasons I fell for her.

CHAPTER 6:
LOVE AND MARRIAGE

On May 6, 2005, less than 10 months after we met, we married. In the days leading up to the wedding I started to develop cold feet. I was nervous about tying the knot again, and I began to doubt myself. Christina noticed the change in my behavior and feared that I was going to back out at the last minute. It was a valid concern, but ultimately I knew my life would never be complete without her.

Christina planned the perfect wedding at Arroyo Trabuco Golf Course in Mission Viejo, California. The venue's outdoor wedding garden provided a beautiful backdrop for what Christina later described as "the happiest day of my life."

The day of the wedding was emotional for Christina. Her parents divorced when she was very young, and it was the first time they had all been in the same room in many years. She was comforted, knowing that her family was there. While Christina was in the bridal suite anxiously awaiting her time to walk down the aisle, I was just as nervous standing before 200 of our friends and family. The moment the doors leading out to the venue opened up and the music started playing, Christina looked me in the eyes and everything fell into place. A calmness settled over me the closer she got, and when she finally took my hands it was only the two of us. No one else was in my peripheral vision and we said our vows locked in each other's gaze. I was mesmerized by her beauty and eager to spend the rest of my life with her.

The evening was one I will always remember. The smile Christina wore the entire night made my heart feel light. One of the most memorable moments of the reception was our first dance. We had all the guys from the Tijuana Dogs performing for most of the evening, myself included, but in between sets people danced to a playlist we had put together on a CD. When it was time for the first dance, I got up on stage with the band and started singing "The Way You Look Tonight" by Frank Sinatra. As Christina approached the stage, I stepped down and held her in my arms and we swayed to the melody. It became our song.

We settled into married life very easily. Christina graduated college with a degree in Early Childhood Education from California State University Fullerton a few weeks after we said "I Do." From there she transitioned from working for her family's insurance company to working as an assistant at a private school called Pegasus. Meanwhile I was teaching at Harbor Day School in Corona Del Mar and coaching the eighth-grade boys' basketball team. Christina would usually come out and attend practices. In true Christina fashion, she often shouted pointers at the players while standing behind me.

"Get your feet moving! Get those hands up!" she would scream. I was embarrassed at first, but Christina really knew what she was talking about and wasn't afraid to express her opinions. Being around her was like hanging out with my buddies. She was just so cool.

One night, I had a Tijuana Dogs performance that conflicted with a game. I asked Christina if she could coach the team.

"Sure," she said, and handled it.

The athletic director called me the next day, saying, "Christina really knows her stuff!" He was in the process of looking for another P.E. coach and was so impressed by Christina's talent that he went to the headmaster of the school and lobbied for her. Soon, she was hired.

Our lives were now fully synchronized. We worked together at school, and we collaborated on band logistics, booking, and the actual shows. I sometimes wondered if it would be too much. There is such a thing as spending too much time with someone, and we were together almost all day every day. But it never got old.

We would talk about people and work. We liked to talk about sports and music. We never ran out of things to discuss, and we always had each other's backs.

Playing shows on the weekends was a regular occurrence, and oftentimes I'd be swamped with grading papers and prepping for the school week as well. Christina would come in and spend hours helping me get everything done in time. She took charge without any complaint. We were a team. All I had to do was teach or be a lifeguard, work with my band on the weekends, and Christina did the rest. I cannot emphasize enough how much she did.

At school, our chemistry became clear. We took our lunch breaks together, and our coworkers would say that when the Mausers came into the teachers' lounge, they knew it was going to be a fun afternoon.

If I had a period off, I would walk down to the gym where she was teaching and she'd have the kids running laps, so I'd run around in circles with them in my suit and tie and do leaps through the air to give them all a laugh. We just really had fun together.

The once reluctant bachelor was now fully domesticated in every aspect of life, and loving every minute of it.

My dad still marvels at the change: "When Matt married Christina, he focused all his energy on one human being. That's what marriage is and he was devoted to it."

Then came the babies. Three years after we got married, Penelope came along, then two years later, Thomas, then Ivy, six years later. The life I was sure I never wanted was more fulfilling than I ever expected.

Christina embraced motherhood in a way that was awe-inspiring. She created such a loving, safe environment at home and took on the day-to-day care for the kids with the same energy and excitement she put into everything she did. She made multitasking look like child's play. She'd be changing diapers and scheduling band performances all while cooking dinner. She ran the household, worked at school, managed the band, and still made time for date nights, friends, vacations, and extended family get-togethers.

"I remember we took a trip to New York in 2019," Penny reflects. "My dad and my brother and my sister were walking ahead of us, and it was just me and Mom. We were looking at the buildings, discussing architecture, and Mom put her arm around me. I remember feeling completely safe, surrounded by a wonderful, warm feeling."

Christina made everyone feel that way. She was the conductor of the orchestra of our lives. I never made lunch. Everything was organized. The band was thriving, and I got to spend every day with my wife, and then our kids ended up going to school with us too. This was the best time of my life.

In 2011, while performing with the Tijuana Dogs, I kept noticing local tribute bands performing acts like Queen and Journey. I recalled my mom telling me how I sounded just like Frank Sinatra, so I called my friend Pete Jacobs, who was a big band director, and said, "We should do Sinatra. Nobody is doing that."

Pete agreed, and we launched a project called the Sinatra Big Band. I didn't give much thought into whether we were unique or special until we performed at weddings. We would play a dinner set and people would say, "Oh my God, you sound just like Sinatra!" Within a year or two, our Sinatra Big Band took off with Christina at the helm of management duties.

Photo Credit: Pala Casino

CHAPTER 7:
HERE COMES THE BOOM

In 2015 both the Sinatra Big Band and Tijuana Dogs were running on autopilot. We were booked over 100 days per year, and in high demand. The gigs themselves were pretty routine, but being innovative and having a creative outlet has always been an important part of my music career. In my desire to stay in a creative headspace, I invented a character by the name of Vladimir Boom, which was so far out in left field, that it proved to be a shining example of how insanely supportive Christina was.

My brother, Gabe, had a Brazilian friend who used to always say, "Let's make party!" whenever he was looking to have a good time, and I thought, *Hey, that's a song!* So I went and wrote the song and somehow, when my creative juices started flowing, I decided that the song had to be sung by a Russian guy who spoke English with an accent. Then I realized that it couldn't just be a song, because no one would get it. I came up with the idea to create an entire character – a Russian who really loved America – to sell the song and bring it to life. I named him "Vladimir Boom," and invented an entire backstory to support his existence. Initially I thought it was hilarious, but the more I thought about it the more I started to second-guess myself, so I pitched it to Christina.

In a long, drawn out speech, I explained his background and motives to her: Boom was born near Chernobyl and he moved all over Russia with his gypsy family growing up. He developed a passion for making music and made it to Moscow as an adult, where he started a nightclub called The Boom Shelter, which was an abandoned bomb shelter. He became the biggest nightclub owner in Moscow, and everybody loved him. An American girl named Anna came to his club one day, and he fell in love. After a whirlwind romance that was cut short when Anna's father decided to move his family back to the U.S., he was devastated. He decided to leave Russia and start fresh in America. His objective was to establish himself as a pop star and show the greatest country in the world "The Boom!" He tried to come across on a freighter, but they denied him entry because he was illegal, so he made his way to Mexico and successfully crossed the border to the U.S. illegally. He quickly made friends, worked a fast food job, cut lawns, fixed cars, and did whatever he could to make it. He never gave up.

Christina sat and listened with a big smile on her face the entire time as I rambled on and on about Boom. When I was done, she said to me, "*You* are Vladimir Boom. Don't give up. Let's do it!"

"Yeah, but it's stupid," I replied. "People might not get the humor in it all."

"Are you crazy? Who cares what other people think?" she countered. "Just do it and don't worry about it. You have to pursue these ideas."

I said, "Alright, then. Let's do it!"

She laughed, telling me, "This is why I married you. I didn't want a boring life. I wanted to have fun, and everything you do is fun."

Encouraged by her support, I went on to write several songs as "Vladimir Boom." Most of the lyrics were so ridiculous and outlandish that I didn't think even Christina would like them. But she did. She even sang background vocals for one of them. There were two songs whose music videos I could picture in my head right off the bat, so I got to work outlining the visuals and creating storyboards. Christina took over production of the videos, casting, and organizing the film schedule. We had a blast with it.

As a team, Christina and I just got stuff done. We didn't over analyze anything, we just did whatever it was we came up with and if we liked it, great – if we didn't, we made adjustments. It was very rare where we'd stop and go, "You're so great…you're so amazing…" We were busy living and enjoying life. The fact that we were supporting each other was all we needed. We didn't fawn over one another, we just got things done – it was how we showed we cared.

The morning of the "Let's Make Party" video shoot, one of the girls who was supposed to star in it backed out. Without missing a beat, Christina was on the phone and had another girl there within the hour. The shoot was a riot. We laughed so hard during filming that we had to retake several scenes. When we saw the finished product, we doubled over in a fit of laughter.

Let's Make Party

She posted the video to our YouTube channel and it took some time to get traction, but within a few months the students who attended the school we taught at got wind of it and the views skyrocketed nearly overnight. The kids all started sharing it, telling their friends, "This is my teacher!"

One of the other teachers pulled me aside and said, "One of the parents called and complained about a teacher who was in an inappropriate video that was posted online." That's when the principal pulled me in. It was so embarrassing. I walked into her office and she turned her computer monitor toward me, and I saw the "Let's Make Party!" video fill the entire screen.

"What's this?" she asked.

"This is a side job," I said.

She wasn't amused. At all. She even threatened me with legal action. Christina and I had to consult with lawyers to make sure we didn't do anything really wrong. Ultimately, the principal was adamant about taking it down. "It's either this video, or your job," she said with conviction. So I shut up, took the video off YouTube, and put Vladimir Boom on the back burner.

When the Tijuana Dogs and Sinatra Big Band got so big that I finally had to quit teaching, I gave the principal a Vladimir Boom t-shirt and Christina re-posted the video online.

Long live The Boom.

Pinche Guerro

CHAPTER 8:
BEFRIENDING A G.O.A.T.

When our children became school-age, we enrolled them at Harbor Day so they could be close to us. We had a good 10 years with our family together around the clock. Christina and I coached the seventh and eighth grade boys' and girls' basketball teams together, we coached track together, we took family leaves together, we did family vacations. We had an exceptional, fun family. My heart was full.

And then the most surreal thing happened: I became friends with Kobe Bryant.

One of the least glamorous aspects about teaching is managing the drop-off and pick-up line, before and after school. It is a form of organized chaos, and maintaining the steady flow of traffic for maximum efficiency and safety for the children is the most important part of the job.

The first time I crossed paths with Kobe Bryant, I was on line duty. I watched as he stopped in the middle of the drop-off line, got out of his car, and casually strolled into the school. I knew I had to keep the line moving, but as a lifelong Los Angeles Lakers fan, I wasn't about to voluntarily do something that might irk or annoy one of the greatest basketball players in NBA history. I was a little starstruck, but duty called. The headmaster approached me and said, "Go get him. He's blocking all the cars."

I found him inside and said, "Mr. Bryant, you have to move your car."

He replied, "Oh, sorry, no problem," and moved his car without incident or complaint, though an extensive line had formed behind him. But for the first time in my experience on line duty, no one seemed to mind as Kobe smiled and waved to everyone he was blocking.

For the first couple of years, we would see each other around school or at school events, and exchange pleasantries in passing. Kobe was an extremely polite and well-mannered man. I had to check my Lakers fan hat at the door whenever I was in his presence to maintain a level of professionalism. There were other famous athlete-parents and celebrity parents whose children attended the school: Jim Abbott, a former Major League pitcher, was always around and was a great guy; Scotty Brooks, who was a longtime NBA coach, had children in the school too; the Lakers' General Manager, Rob Pelinka, had his children in the school. There were many accomplished business people like Bill Gross (the founder of PIMCO), and wealthy families there. Some had more than others, but wealth or status in life did not matter – their children's education was the priority. It did, however, make for a very interesting work environment.

In 2015, Kobe's daughter, Natalia, was in one of my classes. Kobe and I would speak from time to time and became acquainted on a superficial level.

That same year, my Sinatra Big Band played at one of the school's fundraisers. Kobe attended the show, and afterward he walked up and said, "Man, you guys are amazing. You sound just like Sinatra." He seemed genuinely impressed, which was pretty cool. The more I came to know Kobe, the more I realized he was sincerely appreciative of people who were good at what they did.

Unfortunately for Kobe and the Lakers, he hurt his shoulder that year and was out for the rest of the season rehabilitating his injury. Kobe had time on his hands and began to hang around the school a little more. I was preparing to take a group of students from my Spanish class, including Natalia Bryant, on an all-day field trip to San Diego when Kobe asked if he could join me as a chaperone. I answered with an emphatic, "Yes."

On the bus, Kobe sat right next to me. I struck up a conversation with him, asking if he knew anything about where we were going in San Diego, and he admitted that he didn't. I explained Mission San Diego, where we were headed, was the original site where Catholic Father Junipero Serra started his missions in 1769 to secure what is now California for Spain. We discussed Old Town and San Diego as a busy shipping port. Kobe was intrigued, mentioning that his knowledge of history was mostly European history, because he grew up in Italy.

I could sense Kobe was an extremely intelligent guy, and he talked about his passions in an almost childlike manner. He had so much enthusiasm. Most people are guarded and usually do not reveal intense passion when talking about something, but Kobe was a keen listener with an innate curiosity about things.

We discussed how Christina had snapped her Achilles tendon a couple of weeks prior in a basketball game. Kobe had suffered the exact same injury during his career with the Lakers, so he provided some tips on how to get her back on her feet. The conversation continued to flow freely until we arrived in San Diego. Once we had the kids lined up with their tour guides, he and I hung in the back and continued our conversation from the bus.

When the tour guides took the kids to lunch, Kobe and I sat together at a separate table. A crowd began to assemble outside to gawk at Kobe. Used to, and immune from the commotion, Kobe opened up and started talking about basketball. We discussed his relationships with Phil Jackson, Shaquille O'Neal, and Michael Jordan – it was a thoroughly engaging conversation. Having been a Lakers fan since 1980 when Magic Johnson came in, I knew almost everything about the team.

The stories he was telling me were ones I already knew, but it was like getting a play-by-play from the inside – from the guy I watched make history himself. As a history and sports buff, it was a

Top 10 moment in my life. *Unreal*, I remembered thinking. I had to keep reminding myself that I was still working, and to check in on the kids every once in a while.

Kobe said Phil Jackson was a genius, and described confronting Jordan in a game to try to take down his idol. He also spoke of philosophical subjects, mostly about how to face your heroes. Kobe described how he would get Shaquille O'Neal fired up, because in his observation, when Shaq was pissed, he was a beast. I was fully invested in the conversation. It didn't feel like a fan talking to a superstar; it was simply two guys discussing topics of legendary status where one happened to have the inside scoop. "Kobe," I said to him. "I've got to tell you, man, it's crazy being able to pick your brain about all this stuff." He smiled and shrugged it off.

By this time, he was comfortable discussing different players whom he liked or disliked. Kobe was very frank and honest. Knowing I was a musician, Kobe turned the tables. He began to ask me a multitude of questions about my music. He wanted to hear some of the music I had composed and performed because he was considering forming his own production company when his basketball career was over.

On the bus ride back to school, we had a good two-hour conversation about music. Kobe loved Michael Jackson, The Beatles, The Rolling Stones. He liked many genres of music. Kobe loved John Williams and theatrical music. He loved plays – one of his favorite musicals was *Mary Poppins*. Kobe told me he personally knew Julie Andrews, who is synonymous with the character Mary Poppins, and he spoke about how he wanted to start his own production company to, in part, produce musical shows. He asked me to send him some music samples; luckily I had several songs I had written stored on my cell phone and played them for him.

I would play Kobe a song, and he would listen to it intently and study it. Watching him process information was remarkable.

Appearing deeply in thought, he soaked it in completely, dedicating his full attention. We had the most intense conversation. It started at 7 a.m., and it did not end until I got the kids off the bus at 3 p.m. For eight hours, we talked about everything. At one point in the conversation, I asked him if he was afraid to die. I don't know how the conversation got so deep, but he looked at me with conviction and said, "No. When I die, I'm going to die a beautiful death." He asked me if I'd ever read Japanese poetry. I told him not really, joking that the extent of my knowledge in that area consisted of the occasional Haiku in high school. He told me to look into Japanese poetry because they talked a lot about death as a beautiful part of life. I didn't know what he meant at the time, but it seems so ironic that we even broached the subject.

As we were pulling into the school and getting ready to get the kids off the bus, Kobe looked me in the eye and said, "Matt, what the fuck are you doing teaching? You need to be doing music full-time. I am going to start putting you to work."

I explained that I needed to make a living. The bands were doing great, but with three kids and a wife, we needed the benefits. Kobe mentioned a project he was conceptualizing, and wanted to see if I was interested in collaborating with him. We agreed to give it a trial run. Kobe started sending me songwriting ideas, like sports scenarios, and I would compose songs.

I developed the lyrics, the music, and the melody. Sometimes he had a rough melody that I would have to put to music, and he'd have words. I just massaged whatever he'd send me.

One day, Kobe said he was doing this project for ESPN called *Kobe Bryant's Musecage*. It was based upon animated videos, with Kobe and a puppet called *Little Mamba*. The idea of a "musecage" was finding "musings," or things that you use for motivation.

Kobe believed that tapping into your dark side (he called them "dark musings") generates anger, and energy subsequently required to be a talented player. Kobe sent me a song intended for this project, but it was really rough.

I told him, "Kobe, let me rewrite this for you." He agreed, and used what I wrote in the video.

One day while having my hair cut, the phone rang and "Kobe Bryant" flashed up on the screen. My barber was stunned and I said, "I have to take the call." I jumped out of the chair and answered immediately.

"Hey man, I need you to record that song you wrote," Kobe said. "Can you meet me at the airport in a few hours? We'll take the helicopter to Burbank and you can start recording."

I said, "OK – it's my birthday, so I have to rearrange some things."

"Great," he said. "I'll buy you a cake."

I finished getting my haircut, then rushed home to get ready. I arrived at John Wayne Airport in Orange County, where Kobe and his pilot met me by the helicopter. "Let's get to work," he said, and patted my back as we climbed in.

On the way, he showed me points of interest around L.A. and told a few stories about being on the Lakers, and his routine when he'd fly in for a game or practice. When we landed in Burbank, a limo picked us up from the airport and took us to the studio where, as promised, Kobe had a birthday cake waiting for me. I recorded the song, then watched as he had a children's chorus come in and sing their parts to incorporate into the song.

Kobe appreciated the fact that I could compose a piece in a day – or in an hour sometimes. When he wanted it done, I got it done. Sometimes Kobe was stoked about what I'd created as-is. If he wasn't feeling it, he would say, "rewrite this," or "let's go in a different direction." We developed a very honest and straightforward working relationship as you would in sports, like a teammate. We worked our butts off.

About a year or so later, Kobe started working on a podcast called *The Punies*. The premise of the podcast was to capture conversation from an eclectic group of neighborhood friends who are athletes and take on adventures together. *The Punies* featured original songs and an unforgettable cast of characters known as The Good Ol' Gang. Each episode relied upon important life lessons about how to play with joy and limitless imagination. *The Punies* sought to educate people about the way sports should be played.

Kobe hired Jon Haller to write the scripts and develop storylines, which included lyrics for *The Punies*, and I'd put his lyrics to music. Other times, I would come up with the words.

I wrote a plethora of songs for the series in a matter of two seasons. We would complete them in a month or two. My life became two months of constant writing and writing and writing. I would be at the piano for hours upon hours. The project was fun, but it was a lot of work. Kobe didn't mess around. It was tough, but I loved it.

We built a special little team. I enlisted musicians who worked hard, and he respected that. Kobe brought in musicians such as Dieter Ruehle, the organist for the Dodgers, who could not believe how fast we were producing such great material.

Kobe saw my strength, which was to be creative and develop ideas, and he drew on that in our work. He was effective in recognizing people with talent and incorporating their various abilities to the benefit of the team.

Kobe tapped into my swimming expertise when he was writing one of his children's books called *Geese Are Never Swans*. The book is about a young swimmer who overcomes grief on the road to becoming an Olympian. Kobe, Gigi, and I went to a swim meet in Irvine when the U.S. Nationals were being held. I knew a lot of the people there, including a former lifeguard friend of mine who was the CEO of USA Swimming, Tim Hinchey. Prior to our arrival, I texted Tim that I was bringing a buddy to the event, but failed to mention that the "buddy" was Kobe Bryant. When we showed up, and Tim saw Kobe with me, he had a look of shock and said, "Is that your buddy?"

"Yeah," I said with a smile. We went to the VIP area, where he sat me with the writer of *Geese are Never Swans*, Eva Clark, to go over everything I knew about swimming. While Eva and I were talking about the subtleties of the different strokes and who to watch during each race, Kobe stopped and struck up a conversation with Michael Phelps a few tables away. After a while, he waved me over.

"Matt, this is Michael," he said as he gestured to one of the greatest swimmers of all time. He turned to Michael and said, "Matt's a great swimmer." I shook my head in total embarrassment. "We're not even in the same league, man." I shook Michael's hand and quickly dismissed myself from the conversation. I was not ready to sit there and shoot the shit with two G.O.A.T.s at the same time.

It was 2018, and I was at another interesting place in life: a teacher by day while creating music for Kobe Bryant, playing shows with my bands, and spending time with my family during my time off. It was everything and more than I ever envisioned for myself. Christina made it all possible with her organizational skills to help us all juggle the day-to-day responsibilities and the business of the bands. I was working multiple jobs, and she was, too. Looking back it seems impossible, but Christina made everything run.

Meanwhile, Christina and I were still coaching the girls' and boys' basketball teams at Harbor Day School. Kobe's daughter Gigi, who was in fourth or fifth grade, was starting to get serious about basketball. I told him, "Hey man, if you want to help me out, you have an open invitation anytime."

He called me two days later and said, "Let's put on a basketball camp."

We had a hunch that Kobe wanted to start a girls' club team because of Gigi's growing interest in the sport. We worked on basketball together for about a year while Gigi was on the team. When he saw how much Gigi was enjoying basketball and the hard work she was putting into her game, sure enough, he started his own club team.

We had no clue that this would have a profound impact on the rest of our lives.

CHAPTER 9:
A LIFE-CHANGING DECISION

In fall of 2018, Kobe decided he needed a woman alongside him to coach the girls' club team he had created. He called me out of the blue and asked, "Would Christina want to coach? Does she know a zone defense?" He knew Chrisina was an athlete and coached basketball at Harbor Day, but what he didn't know was the extent of her familiarity with the sport.

While I was on the phone with Kobe, I went to the kitchen where Christina was making dinner and mouthed, "Kobe wants to know if you know a zone defense."

She said, "Of course I know a zone." I put the phone on speaker and relayed her response.

"Would she like to come and show the girls tonight or sometime in the next day or so?" he asked.

She nodded at me and waved her finger in an arch to signify that tomorrow would be better for her, so I told Kobe it was a deal. "She's phenomenal," I added.

"OK, we'll bring her out and let's see how she does." He ended the call.

I looked at Christina and a huge smile spread across my face. She looked back at me, dismayed, and said, "I've got a lot on my plate right now."

"You're going to rock it," I replied. She shook her head and went back to making dinner.

Kobe held practice nearby at the Newport Coast Gym. Christina and I arrived at the gym about a half hour before practice began so she could get the lay of the land before jumping in.

Kobe walked up to us and got right to it. "I'll coach the offense, and you'll coach defense." He introduced Christina to the girls, then turned her loose. "If you have any questions, let me know."

I stepped out for coffee and to run a few errands, and returned after an afternoon of practice. While Christina was talking to some of the girls, Kobe walked over to me, amped by Christina's performance: "Christina really knows the game! She knows how to run it. She knows angles, she knows hand placement. She knew the ins and outs of each position in the zone."

"I told you, man!" I replied, pride swelling in my chest.

On the drive home I could see Christina was replaying the events of the day in her head, trying to process what coaching the team would mean. "It could be too much to handle," she finally said.

I turned to her and said, "Look, he hasn't asked you to commit to anything yet so let's see what his next move is. Don't worry about it. If he asks you to coach, we'll cross that bridge when we get there."

We arrived at that bridge more quickly than either one of us anticipated. Kobe texted me an hour after we returned home from practice and made Christina an offer to coach with him three days a week.

She put her head back, closed her eyes, and took a deep breath. She exhaled slowly, opened her eyes and looked at me. "I do not want to do it," she said with conviction. "I see how demanding he is on you, and I don't want that kind of stress in my life. I've got three kids of my own to take care of and I don't want to be pulled in a million different directions."

I tried to encourage her, "It's an unbelievable opportunity to do something you're exceptionally good at! Just try it and see where it goes. You're the one in control. If it ends up being too much, then step back." She shook her head and put her hands on her hips, but said nothing more.

I messaged Kobe, letting him know she was undecided. He replied immediately with, "I'll talk to her." The next day he called us and explained to Christina and I his vision of how Christina would coach the defense and he would coach offense. He felt strongly that the girls needed a solid female role model and Christina was a prime candidate. She looked up at me and sighed.

"Fine," she conceded. "I'll try it."

In retrospect, I should have listened to her.

By the end of 2018, Christina and I were both still teaching at Harbor Day School, but we were also firmly in Kobe's orbit. Our relationship with him became a working one. We transitioned from being acquaintances, to a parent-teacher relationship, to both Christina and I being on his payroll.

I was already accustomed to Kobe's legendary focus and drive for perfection – elements of his personality that made him one of the greatest basketball players in history – but Christina was not. She knew going in that it was going to be a challenge, so she braced herself for what was to come. She rose to the occasion, as she did in all her endeavors, and Kobe was so impressed by Christina's coaching ability that he soon gave her more responsibilities.

We were so busy that we decided it was time for a change. We had to re-evaluate our lives, recognizing that we were no longer able to juggle everything on our plates. Christina was especially stretched thin.

"I have three kids, I'm running both of your bands, we're teaching, and I'm running this house. It is too much." Adding coaching to the mix only complicated things more.

We came to the conclusion that I could make a living from performing with the bands and working with Kobe, which was also creatively satisfying. I decided to quit my teaching job of 20 years with plans to move the kids to a public school closer to our home, and take on more responsibilities around the house.

A few days after I made the decision, Christina came to my office at school and said, "If you're not going to be here, and the kids aren't going to be here, I don't want to be here without you." She began to cry and said she felt like she would be letting me down since we would lose our benefits. I remember that moment so intensely because I rarely saw her break down.

I put my arm around her and said, "Christina, I am your biggest fan. I am so proud of you. If you need to quit, then quit. I don't want you to be stressed. We'll figure it out." It was one of the most pivotal moments in our relationship. She had supported me for so many years, and here was my chance to support her. It was definitely another moment of clarity in my life. We walked into the administration offices and resigned together.

It was the beginning of a beautiful time in our lives: Penny and Thomas were in school all day and we had Ivy, who was under the age of two at that time. We did not have to commute anymore. We would drop the older two kids off at school, get a bagel, talk basketball or about our plans for the future. We became even closer than we already were after having worked and lived together over the past 10 years.

When Christina told Kobe that she had quit teaching, it became a license for him to go into overdrive. He responded, "Great, even better. Now we can really focus on making this team unstoppable."

Christina was managing the bands, being a mom, and now, had her coaching job. She was totally on board. She said the schedule would allow her to do things with the kids during the day and take them to their after school activities. Her coaching commitment was only from 6:30-8:30 p.m. Each night I would supervise the kids and she would go to work and come right home. She had all day to be with us, since I was mainly working with the bands on the weekends. We had these two beautiful years of spending everyday together, and being able to go to the kids' school activities. Christina was elated, and she got to dedicate even more time to doing what she was really good at – coaching basketball.

Christina had an analytical brain. She learned the most dominant offensive attack, the Triangle offense, in a day. She knew where the ball should go. She knew who should be cutting. She knew who should be setting screens for whom. We would watch Lakers games and Christina would break them down. She was methodical in everything she did. I always told her she should have become a lawyer. Whenever we would get in an argument, Christina would have facts and figures and remember dates of what I said, when I said it, and how I said it. It didn't always work in my favor. She had an amazing mind.

Within a few months, Kobe realized the girls were losing games because some of the hardcore club teams devoted much more time to practice. Kobe's competitive fire was lit, and, as usual, he was driven to win. Overnight, the practice schedule went from three days a week to almost every day.

Kobe pulled out all the stops. He would bring in guest coaches such as God Shammgod, a former NBA point guard and a current NBA coach, as a dribbling specialist. Kyrie Irving came in, Pau Gasol, Jayson Tatum, Kawhi Leonard, and Lakers coaches like Phil Handy would come to work with the girls.

The team would sometimes travel to tournaments in private planes, but Christina hated to fly. *Hated* it. I got a text message from her one day while she was at the airport saying, "I wish you were here. I hate flying." The team had one bumpy landing that scared her so much she almost didn't want to coach anymore. But Christina pushed through it because air travel was not that frequent. She took five or six trips on private planes when the team would travel out of state, and maybe four other trips in the helicopter with the team.

Kobe hoped to assume coaching the girls' basketball program at Sage Hill, a local private school, and they were going to bring all the girls from the club team. On the team was NBA great, Zach Randolph's daughter, McKenna, herself a talented player who is now an All-American at University of Louisville. All the competitive young girls came to play for Kobe – this club team was going to be his dynasty.

Christina was part of developing Kobe's club team from the ground floor. I remember glancing at her on the couch one night as she was watching television, and an overwhelming sense of gratitude washed over me. "You know how unbelievably proud of you I am, right?" I asked, moving closer to her on the couch. "You've been supporting me and our family for so long…and now you're an accomplished, widely respected basketball coach. You're incredible." She became teary-eyed and laid her head on my chest. I wrapped my arms around her, kissed the top of her head, and held her. It was such a beautiful, private moment.

The basketball girls called Christina the "Mother of Defense." She was extremely proud of her team and loved coaching the girls. Kobe respected her ability and let her work independently during games and in practice. She felt like she had earned his respect. Christina was a trusted assistant alongside a legend, and it was amazing to watch her grow.

At home, music filled the house, just like I had always wanted. My band's shows were a family affair. Tom played multiple instruments and liked to sing and dance during our concerts. He even did a music video for a song he and I wrote called "Busted."

Busted

Ivy was quite little, but she loved to sing along and dance as well. Penny is a beautiful singer with the confidence to stand in front of large crowds and perform. She and I also wrote a song together called "Green Bike" that we were excited to sing on stage together. It is a classic call-and-response song about a parent's worry for their child, who is out riding her favorite bike, oblivious to the harsh realities of the world. As Penny sang about feeling the ocean breeze and breaking into song while cruising carelessly for hours, I sang about my concerns:

> *I know you're feeling independent*
> *Every little rule you want to bend it*
> *Can you just hold on for a year or two?*
> *Where are you going when you're not in our sights?*

It was a catchy song, and we made plans to debut it during a sold-out Sinatra Big Band show at The Brea Improv on January 26, 2020.

Green Bike

On January 25, 2020, I had a show at a car museum in Orange County by John Wayne Airport. Christina came by to see me. She helped me unload equipment, then we perused the antique cars commenting on the designs of each one. When I walked her to her car, I remember giving her a big kiss and telling her that I loved her. The kids were at home sick with the nanny, and she was exhausted. She looked at me with tired eyes, and told me that we needed to reconnect because we'd been so busy lately. I wholeheartedly agreed, and we made plans to spend time together in the coming week. As we said goodbye, I let her know I'd be home late because of the show, and she said she'd wait up.

I got home around midnight and found Christina playing with Ivy on the bed, laughing and making goofy faces while Ivy giggled. I vividly remember thinking, *God, my little girl's so lucky to have such a loving mom.*

I got ready for bed and laid down next to my wife. She gave me a kiss and turned out the light. "Penny still isn't feeling very well, so I'm wondering if I should take her with me tomorrow," she said, referring to the flight she had to take aboard the helicopter to a tournament in Thousand Oaks. Penny played on one of the younger teams at Kobe's academy, and she, too, had a game the next day.

"Let's keep her home so she can rest," I told Christina. Little did I know that this simple decision would save my daughter's life.

"I agree," she said as she shifted to her side with her head on the pillow and looked at me. "I can't wait to see you and Penny perform 'Green Bike' at the show tomorrow night. You guys are going to be great."

I rolled to my side, facing her, and brushed a strand of hair from her eyes with my finger. "I'm excited too."

"I'm getting up early so I'll try not to wake you," she said as she yawned. "I'll be back by noon, so I'll have plenty of time to do Penny's hair and help her get ready for the show."

"Sounds good," I said as I closed my eyes. "Sweet dreams."

CHAPTER 10:
A LIFE SHATTERED

I woke up on January 26, 2020, to the feel of Christina's lips pressed against my own. "Love you," I heard her whisper as she walked out of our bedroom. I was groggy, and mumbled a barely audible "Love you, too," but she was already gone. This was the start of the worst day of my life.

Our wonderful nanny, Alma, was at the house early because I needed to get some rest. When I finally got up for the day at around 10 a.m., I checked my phone for messages from Christina. She *always* texted me when she landed because of her fear of flying. Always. "I am here. I am safe. I love you." But there was nothing. I texted her, asking if everything was OK, and waited for a response. As the minutes ticked by with no reply, I kept telling myself there was probably a delay with the flight and she was just wrapped up in handling whatever the situation was. But a big part of me knew she would have told me if that was the case – if there had been a change in plans. So I texted her again, saying that she was starting to worry me and to text me and let me know she was OK.

I heard a knock at my bedroom door, and Alma called through the door, "Christina said for me to keep an eye on Ivy because she's running a bit of a fever."

"OK, I'm getting ready and I'll be out in a second," I told her.

A minute or two later I got a call from Chuck Finley, the former baseball star for Major League Baseball's Angels. He said he wanted to come to my show that evening but that it was sold out. I was distracted for a little bit while I called the Improv to check on adding him to the guest list. As I hung up the phone, I checked my messages again and there was still nothing from Christina. My gut was telling me that there was definitely something wrong, and my stomach started doing backflips.

Then, another call came through. It was my big band director, Pete Jacobs. "Is Christina OK?" The anxiety in his voice made me nervous.

"Why?" I asked tentatively.

"Because Kobe's dead."

My body went numb as my mind put the pieces together. At that moment I knew the helicopter had crashed. I knew Christina was dead. No question. I hung up the phone, fell to my knees, both of my hands pulling at my hair, and let out the most primal scream that shook me to my core. I started to rock back and forth, trying to wrap my head around the fact that I would never see my wife again. My kids were going to grow up without a mother.

Then I began rationalizing everything. *I'm going to be OK. We're going to be OK. We'll figure this out.* It all went through my mind in a flash.

My kids, I thought.

I pulled myself up off the floor and tried to compose myself so I could be an anchor for my children when I broke the news. *How do I tell them that mommy's never coming home?*

I emerged from my room in a daze and balanced against the hallway wall before staggering forward a few steps. I placed a hand on the wall, my legs heavy and unsteady, and took several deep breaths before I reluctantly made my way to the living room, where I found Penny and Tom sitting on the couch watching TV. As I stood behind the couch, watching them watch the screen, for several moments I just took in the sight of them. Something on the program they were watching made them giggle and I felt a tightness grip my chest, knowing it was probably the last time I'd hear them laugh so effortlessly in the foreseeable future. I tried to hold onto those final moments of normalcy before I turned their entire world upside down.

"Penny, Tom, I need you to turn off the television please. Daddy needs to talk to you," I said, voice cracking. I walked around the front of the couch, and crouched down in front of both of them. They looked at me with curiosity, noting the seriousness in my tone. I took Penny's hand and reached for Tom's as well, and gave them a tight squeeze. Inhaling deeply, I chose my words carefully.

"There's been an accident…and mommy is gone. Mommy died. She is in heaven with the angels now," I managed to get out. I silently cursed myself for not thinking of some better way to have said it. But was there a better way? The rulebook on parenting goes out the door when you have to tell your children that their mother is never coming home.

I leaned into them as they lunged toward me from their positions on the couch, and held them with a protective fierceness while they sobbed uncontrollably in my arms. If my heart hadn't already been broken by the news of Christina's death, surely this moment was going to kill me. With their heads buried on either side of my neck, I rubbed their backs, trying to console them.

"It's going to be OK," I tried to reassure them. "We're going to be alright." I hardly believed my own words and could only hope that one day it would be true.

At the sound of Penny's and Tom's cries, Alma walked into the living room with Ivy in her arms and a concerned look in her eyes. As I relayed the news of Christina's death, the wailing grew louder and then all five of us were in tears. I took Ivy from Alma and sat back down on the couch, holding all three of my babies for dear life.

Eventually I pulled back, then one by one I took their precious faces in my trembling hands, looked them in the eyes and reiterated that we were going to be OK.

"Daddy has to make some phone calls right now, so stay with Alma and I'll be back in just a little bit." They all huddled together as I headed back to my room so they wouldn't have to hear me repeat the awful news again and again while I notified family and friends of her passing.

The first call I made was to Christina's mom, Tita. The words were barely out of my mouth before her shrill cry pierced through the telephone. Sitting on the corner of my bed with my head in my hands after I got off the phone with Tita, I lost it. I went off in a rage, throwing a chair and kicking the bedside table before succumbing to the sobs that erupted from my chest.

Slowly the sobs subsided, and I picked up the phone again. The next call I made was to my dad.

To this day, he still recalls the conversation vividly: "In a voice I will never forget, Matt said, 'Christina's dead.' I went into a state of shock. I immediately quit my job after hanging up with Matt. I then drove the two hours from my house in the desert to spend three weeks with Matt at his house with his children. When I walked in, I saw how the news had hit him. Matt's pain became another trauma in my life. I understand tragedy and death; I used to work in the funeral business. But there was my son, strong, powerful, on top of the world. And then the world came along and hit him with a sledge hammer. Suddenly, Matt's on the floor curled up in a fetal position like a child crying, and my grandchildren and I were comforting him."

Soon there were knocks on my door and people I hadn't seen in years started showing up on my doorstep. I stayed outside and didn't let anyone other than immediate family in the house as more and more people came over, not wanting my children to be even further overwhelmed and traumatized than they already were. I became immersed in a whirlwind of activity. The police came to give a formal notification, then blocked off the cul-de-sac we lived on when the news crews started showing up. When I couldn't take anymore people patting my back, hugging me, and telling me everything was going to be OK, I returned to the house where my family members had gathered and shut down. The rest of the day was a blur.

That night, Alma helped me put the kids to bed, and that's when it started to sink in for Ivy. She was only three at the time, so she knew something was going on and heard that mommy wasn't coming home, but didn't really grasp the fact that she would never see her mother again. While we were trying to get her to sleep, she kept crying over and over: "Where's mommy? I want mommy!"

"She's in heaven, baby," I tried telling her again.

"But she was just here! Where is she? I want her to come home *now*!" she screamed.

"She's not coming home," I said while I held her in my arms until she finally cried herself to sleep. It crushed me. To this day, Ivy has trouble falling asleep on her own and insists upon either myself or one of our nannies being with her until she's asleep.

The next morning I woke up feeling like I'd been run over by a truck. I glanced at my phone to see what time it was, then saw several text messages pop up from various news media outlets.

Christina was one of nine people who were killed in the crash: Kobe Bryant and his 13-year-old daughter, Gianna; pilot Ara Zobayan; John and Keri Altobelli and their 14-year-old daughter Alyssa; and 13-year-old Payton Chester along with her mother, Sarah.

Because of Kobe, this was an international story. The news was running in the living room all day long and it was all "Kobe Bryant and his daughter Gianna died in a helicopter crash," with little mention of the other seven people on board who lost their lives. I wanted my wife's name out there. I wanted her to be remembered, too. When people thought of the helicopter crash that killed Kobe Bryant I wanted them to remember that there were other people who died. I know he's a huge name and an inspiration to so many people across the globe, but my wife was an inspiration to everyone who had the privilege of knowing her. I couldn't speak for the other families who had lost loved ones on that flight, but I knew I could speak about Christina and let the world know what kind of person she was and how dearly she would be missed.

Within two days, I had an interview with Anderson Cooper on CNN. His dad died when he was 10, so he understood just how difficult this situation was with three kids aged three, nine, and 11, who had just lost their mother. It was raw and emotional, but at the same time, an open and honest conversation about grief and his mom's advice about the importance of just trying to wake up each day.

"My mom used to say, 'sometimes all you can do is just put one foot in front of the other, or if you're not feeling like doing that just keep breathing minute by minute or even second by second,'" Anderson told me. "The one thing I always think of about grief, is that it feels really lonely and isolating and it's actually a bond that unfortunately a lot of people share and a lot of people experience. I know it's easy to feel very alone in this right now but there are a lot of people out there who have gone through it and are going through it and I hope you are surrounded by people you can talk to about it." His words hit home.

"The other thing my mom used to say," he continued, "is that there is no timeline for grief...it's obviously different for everybody, and it's never the same, but it gets better."

"It sounds like you had a pretty good mom, Anderson," I told him.

"Yeah, I did. I did," he replied. "Well, your kids have a very good dad." His kind eyes were reassuring, but I felt a kick in my gut as I thought of Christina.

"Well, they had a good mom, too," I said. "A *really* good mom."

Interviews such as the one with Anderson Cooper, began to stack up. They were not easy. I struggled with the difficulties of being in the throes of grief and trying to cope with the suddenness of being a single parent. I wanted people to remember Christina. I wanted to tell our story. In retrospect I was not always up to the task. I was on *Good Morning America* and the *Today* show. When I later listened to the *Today* show interview, I was disappointed at some of my responses. One host asked how I felt, and I wanted to say, "How do you think I feel?" but I regretfully said, "I can't describe how I feel. It's all four-letter words."

The Paséa Hotel in downtown Huntington Beach reached out and gave all of our family members who came to town free rooms for the week after her death. My brother, Nick, flew in from Texas and took over the technical aspect of things. He was really tech-savvy and immediately got on the computer and made a list of all my passwords and dates the bills needed to be paid. Christina was the one who held all our passwords and made sure all the bills were paid on time, and my job was to make the financial decisions. Nick helped me get into all the accounts I needed to get into now that I was on my own.

On February 1, hundreds of people attended a candlelight vigil that was held at Pier Plaza in our hometown of Huntington Beach. Christina, the kids, and I all have deep roots within the community and it was unbelievable to see how many people were affected by her death. Although the kids and I didn't attend, we read about it in the paper and friends told us how beautiful it was. The entire community was pulling together for us and their support became a lifeline, not in the way of fixing anything, but in simply being there, offering comfort without expectation.

The next day, the San Francisco 49ers and the Kansas City Chiefs were playing in the Super Bowl with the world watching. I was sitting at home, trying to stay engaged in the game to get my mind off losing Christina, if only for a few minutes, when they announced her name along with everyone else who lost their lives in the crash on live TV. For a fleeting moment it was as though the world paused to acknowledge her, and I promised myself I would keep her memory alive wherever possible.

On February 15, Christina's alma mater, Edison High School, held a celebration of life for her in the school's gym. The kids and I attended, and it was incredible. The place was filled to the brim with hundreds of friends, former classmates and teammates, teachers, coaches, and countless people whose lives she had touched. Her high school basketball coach, Dave White, was one of the speakers. He made such a poignant speech about the type of person she was and shared some of his memories of her, and those of her former teammates.

"One of the hardest workers I've ever coached was a girl named Christina Patterson," Dave White said. "When your best players are your leaders and hardest workers, you will have a great season and your job as a coach will be easier. She was athletic, quick, could jump, driven, intense, had a killer instinct, was a lockdown defender, and a winner. Sounds like Kobe Bryant. I could see why Kobe wanted Christina to be his top assistant. He saw himself in her. When I heard the Mamba team named her M.O.D. – Mother of Defense – I felt like a proud dad. In basketball, Christina was a four-time varsity letter winner, two-time Hall of Fame winner, and Edison's Athlete of the Year in 1999. I love her, I will miss her, and she will always be a Hall of Famer in my eyes.

"There is a quote I love," Dave told the crowd. "'It's not what you receive in life. It's what you give.' And boy did Christina give. At Edison, Christina was a great player, teammate, and friend. She later became a great teacher, coach, and mentor. But her greatest accomplishment in life was that she was a great daughter, sister, wife, and mother. She was so proud of Matt and her children. Christina told me they were everything to her."

The comments from her former teammates were equally emotional and beautiful to hear:

"Christina taught me what it meant to be a captain, a leader. I feared her because I respected her. I never wanted to let her down. The valuable lessons I learned that year [I played with her] set the foundation for my next three years in high school and beyond." – Rachel

"Christina's leadership and court presence were just as big as her personality. I don't recall her ever giving less than one hundred percent effort and demanding the same from her teammates." – Bianca

"Christina loved to sing and dance. She was infectious and always happy. These moments made me feel young, free, alive, and in each of those moments with her, nothing else mattered. I will forever cherish these times with Christina." – Shauna

"My strongest memory of Christina isn't one moment in time, but a season. We spent the entire 1998 summer in the gym working on our game, challenging each other to get better. I may have been a little intimidated by her – she was pretty and popular and so many things I wasn't. We were teammates bonded by a common goal of winning (and surviving Coach White). We improved our basketball skills that summer and led our teammates to do the same. More importantly, I got to fully know, understand and appreciate the kind, witty, and whip smart Christina. Christina was also a hell of an athlete, a fierce competitor, and a great teammate. She led us to a Sunset League Championship her senior year. Christina never had a problem fitting in, showing up as a confident woman, and making an impact. As a teacher and coach, she positively influenced so many young people in the way she influenced me; leading with compassion and a healthy dose of competition, helping others who may be shy, awkward, or unsure find their voice. I know I am so grateful she did that for me!" – Michelle

Her funeral the next day, on February 16, was something else entirely. It didn't have the same warm, loving feeling that the celebration of life at Edison had. It was held at Christ Cathedral in Garden Grove, and was again packed with hundreds of people mourning the loss of Christina. But from the moment I stepped foot inside the church, I hated every minute of it. It felt all wrong. I feel like Christina would have hated it, too. It wasn't light and uplifting like she was – like how it had been at Edison. Instead, the cathedral, once a place of warmth and reverence, felt cold and hollow. Thick, oppressive silence filled the air, broken only by the faint murmurs of mourners shifting in their seats. Even the organ seemed off-pitch, the guitar out of tune; together, they seemed to echo the despair and heartache of the moment.

I remember seeing her ashes in the urn for the first time there, and I could hardly grasp the reality of it. The person I once held so close was now reduced to something so… final.

We walked up the stairs to the main entrance and I thought, *OK, here we go – just go through the motions and it will all be over soon.* Then I'm holding my kids as we sit in the church, staring at their mom, who's in a *jar.* That was a horrible moment seared in my brain. We sat and listened to the prayers and readings, and heard more speakers tell stories…but I grew frustrated. I appreciated the fact that people were sharing their thoughts about her, but some of the remarks were hard for me to hear. Each speech was a stark reminder that my wife was truly gone.

Before they removed the urn from the church, I reached out to put my hands on it, touching what held the remains of my wife's physical body for the last time. The smooth surface offered no comfort, no connection. My grip tightened for a moment, but I let go, knowing there was nothing but memories left to hold onto. I wept openly, in front of the entire church, with my children at my side.

After we laid her to rest, a quiet sense of finality enveloped me. This was it. This was where life without Christina began.

CHAPTER 11:
NAVIGATING WITHOUT A COMPASS

For weeks, I could not sleep. I was terrified. How was I going to continue without her? How was I going to raise three kids without their mom? I had all these disturbing thoughts about Christina and the way she died. Christina used to wake up from nightmares once or twice a week. She would have these dreams where somebody was chasing her and lighting her on fire. She'd be jolted awake, drenched in a cold sweat and panic-stricken by the images that flooded her mind. I'd hold her and comfort her, repeating "You're OK, you're fine," until the feeling of terror had passed. It was always the same dream: somebody setting her on fire. The tragic irony of her nightmares is impossible to ignore, and haunts me to this day.

I tried to be steady for my kids but I was struggling, blaming myself for everything. Had I not encouraged her to work with Kobe, she would have never been on that helicopter. What did I do wrong? Where did I go wrong? I was going through phases of madness where I felt like I did not know who I was. I would writhe in pain and cry. In some moments I felt like I was floating above my body, watching myself.

I did not know how I was going to do life without her. I had lawyers at my house bringing up difficult subjects and hitting me with an endless lineup of questions, the answers to which I didn't always have. And then there were the funerals for the other victims, many of whom were our family friends. Attending each funeral felt like stepping into an alternate universe – it was a blur of names and faces that slowly blended into one unrecognizable body of grief. There was a constant sense of mourning, of despair, and there was no escape.

I couldn't bring myself to go to Kobe's public memorial service. It happened to fall on my 50th birthday, but that wasn't the reason why. I knew there would be many famous people talking about Kobe, and what an impact he had not only in the sport of basketball, but off the court as well. Hell, he had a huge impact on my life in more ways than one. But I decided it was best to pay my respects to him in my own way, and was at peace with my decision.

I started talk therapy about a week after the accident, and it was torture. One of the obvious questions the therapist asked was, "How do you feel? Tell me about that." Again, it's like, *How the hell do you think I feel? I just lost my wife!* I tried it for two months and had to stop. By forcing me to relive the pain over and over, it was making things so much worse. It wasn't helping. I know talk therapy is an incredible avenue toward healing for so many people, and I'm not speaking out against it whatsoever. It simply wasn't for me.

I called my Masters swimming coach, Diego Pomba, and told him I needed to get back in the pool. We had known each other for years, since my school teaching days, and we usually met at specific times or when he was coaching his teams. Diego is Colombian, and in his thick accent, he spoke of the lane lines that all swimmers focus upon at the bottom of the pool. He said, "I will meet you there. That black line is your therapy." Diego knew exactly what I needed: that silent black line at the bottom of the pool. We did not need to talk; we got in and did our thing.

I knew many people at the pool, and all of them knew my story. I was not ready to mix in with the crowd and answer any questions, or even talk at all. Diego went out of his way to be incredibly gracious and respectful of my mind space.

Diego remembers clearly, "Matt called and told me, 'I am just not ready to start to socialize with many people. Do you mind if we go at a different time?' I replied, 'Absolutely. Tell me when you are ready and I'll go with you.' That's how Matt slowly returned to the water. I asked no questions. He would just say, 'This is rough,' or he would make similar comments. I never tried to dig into anything, only whatever Matt volunteered. When we finished our workout, I'd tell him, 'Hey, anytime.' That was the extent of my talking. I am a coach, so I have these workouts ready. But we did not do anything like that. He just wanted to be mindless in the water. Matt did not have to think about anything. That black line at the bottom of the pool becomes hypnotizing and he just wanted to relieve some of his stress in the water."

The kids accepted talk therapy much better than I did, but I know it was unbelievably difficult for them. "I remember feeling so empty," Penny explains of the weeks after the accident. "I was completely and utterly in denial. And I remember a few days after when I would stare out the window. I would look at the street and there was nothing there. I would wait for my mom to come walking in through the door. People were flooding into the house. People were crying and hugging me, but I could not cry. I just sat there thinking, *This is not real. This is not happening. Mom's coming back.* People were calling me, texting me, writing me notes and letters. And I just could not feel anything. I just read them. And then it got to a point where I shut it out completely. My emotions were gone. I blocked everything and everyone out of my brain. But I had good friends. My two best friends, Jordyn and Sydnee, are twins. They were there for me for the week after Mom passed. We all skipped school. When I returned to school, I did not do any work. I did not want to do any work. I sat in my classes and brought my iPad to school and played video games all day. A classmate asked me one day, 'Who is picking you up? Is your mom coming?' And in dealing with pain and the realization I would never be able to answer 'Yes' to that question again, I said, 'Actually she's not.'

"The pain was just lurking under the surface. I was coping, until I was not, and it came out in the simplest of moments. For example, when I stubbed my toe on my bed, I started bawling. Crying so hard, not because my toe hurt. I did not realize it at the time, but I was just crying because I was so sad and upset. I had all this pent-up emotion that I did not know how to deal with. I just cried for two hours."

We all had our stubbed toe moments. I thank God every day for the friends and family members who came to our aid after everything happened. Christina's family, my family, all of our friends, our nannies – it was incredible. The love and outpouring of support was so powerful. I had people telling me that Charles Barkley and Shaquille O'Neal were raising money for us; that Justin Bieber raised money for us. I had a conversation early on with Vanessa Bryant, Kobe's widow; it was all beyond belief.

As if navigating the depths of grief wasn't enough, life threw us another monumental curveball. I took the kids to school one day, and the administration announced, "We're closing the school on Friday. We're going to be down for two weeks due to COVID-19."

Just as we were learning to live with the loss of Christina, the collective loss of routine, connection, and stability hit us hard— suddenly there was this intense fear of a global pandemic. And, as we all know, those two weeks became substantially longer. Our world shut down. No more support or visits from family and friends; the only people coming over to help were our nannies, Alma and Betty.

There was no more in-person therapy or school for the kids. It was all over Zoom. After a few weeks, the therapy felt impersonal to them and they didn't want to do it anymore. They would sit on Zoom all day for class, then were expected to go another hour sitting in front of a computer for therapy a few times each week. I didn't want to push them through that. Instead, we tried to process our grief as a family unit and made do with what we had.

Between Alma and Betty, I knew the kids were in good hands, even if the grief was inescapable. My coping skills had worn thin amid the isolation. Our house was a short walk to the Santa Ana Riverbed, which is a flood control channel that eventually drains to the ocean. There is a beautiful trail along the river, and I would follow it to the beach and back nearly every day. Most days, the seven-mile round-trip journey wasn't long enough.

One day as I was walking to the trail, it began to rain. It was late March, 2020, and I was surrounded by an eerie quiet, because everything was still shut down due to the pandemic. Everyone was terrified and no one was on the roads. There was this massive fear of the unknown. It was wet and gray and silent, when a car finally approached. For a split second I had this crazy thought: *I'm just going to jump in front of this thing.* The rational part of my brain instantly kicked in, telling me that I still had a life to live, and that the kids had already been through enough. The thought vanished as quickly as it had formed. I reminded myself that things would get better. They *had* to.

That split-second thought was such an abrupt wake-up call. I went home and told myself, *I have got to stay mentally stable. I need to keep writing music to have hope that there is going to be a brighter day.*

Somehow I contracted the COVID-19 virus within those first few weeks of the lockdown, and when the kids got sick, I thought we were all going to die. Our poor nannies, Alma and Betty, got sick as well and couldn't help while they were isolating. I do not know what was worse: being overwhelmed and sick, or being isolated. Tom had a fever of 104 degrees for more than two days and it wouldn't go down – I thought I was going to lose my son. I thought the world was coming to an end. Literally.

Since I couldn't go to the market, we had to order DoorDash for all our meals. That saved us. When we all recovered from COVID, Alma and Betty came back to be with us.

What initially helped me with my grief was going to the studio and writing – but COVID-19 had brought that part of my life to a screeching halt. I could not perform music or go to the studio anymore, but I could still write music on my own. I favored songs of a personal nature. I would sit at the piano, or strum my guitar, and listen to the soothing sounds that brought me to a place of tranquility. Before long, the words began to flow and I found myself writing song after song. I wrote one called "New Life Story," and another called "Lost." I wrote "When You Wake Up and She's Gone." Songwriting served an important purpose in my life, and was the creative outlet I needed to explore and process all my emotions. When the studio reopened, I recorded a music video for "Lost," but in the intro I ended up a blubbering mess. I think it is a beautiful song, but it stirs up so many emotions that I have a hard time listening to it.

Lost

The COVID-19 pandemic was such a harrowing time, only to be compounded by us trying to navigate our own tragic story. But, if Christina were here, it would have been completely different. Our family would have had nothing but time together. For some people, that wouldn't work. For us, we already lived that way. We already had the journey of "life" down pat. Had Christina lived on, we would have had nothing but family time. We might have had another baby.

But the reality was much different than that fantasy. We did our best to limp along through the nightmare that was 2020. When COVID-19 hit our house for the second time, in the fall of 2020, I couldn't believe it. I started feeling neck pain and debilitating muscle aches that would not go away. I felt like I couldn't move.

Penny and Ivy were throwing up, and Tom wasn't doing well, either. I had three kids that were devastatingly ill at the same time, and we were not about to ask Alma or Betty to get sick again, too. We were on our own. That was one of the lowest points of my life.

Once more, DoorDash meal delivery came to our rescue. It was the only way we were able to eat. I would order soup every day. We had already been through so much, and there had been such a deluge of terrible news about the pandemic that we were terrified it was going to kill us all. I remember reading about respiratory distress and having nightmares that Thomas would get a cough, then what? Would I lose him next? They were posting numbers of the rates of infections and fatalities on the news every day. I was weary and tired of the hopelessness I felt.

In certain moments the beauty would seep back in. I thought about "Green Bike" and Penny. I thought about how strange it was that Brea Improv asked me to come back to perform on January 26, 2020, which was only a few months after my previous show there. If we had not booked it, and hadn't made plans to sing together, Penny would've been on that helicopter. That song saved her life.

Of "Green Bike," Penny admits, "It took me a long time to even think about singing 'Green Bike' because I was scared, as I was supposed to go sing it with my father the day my mom died. 'Green Bike' shall be forever linked to losing my mom, so I have had this fear, since losing my mom, that I was going to lose something else – someone else, or that something bad was going to happen. Each time I say goodbye to my dad as he leaves the house, I am terrified to give him a hug goodbye because I am afraid of something happening and losing him."

My kids were obviously grieving, but it showed up in different ways. Penny, outwardly, remained stoic. I remember we watched *SportsCenter* briefly after the accident and saw the outpouring of sorrow. Penny told me it was nice to know everyone else was hurting along with us. Penny is so much like her mother. Tom would shut himself in his room and spend every waking hour doing Speed Cup Stacking. At 10 years old he became the fastest Cup Stacker in the world. Tom became hyper focused on everything he did. He would focus and watch and study. That ability has transferred over to basketball, and now he's an amazing player, just like his mom. Ivy had a lot of anxiety when she started school and whenever she was in new situations. She also had a lot of curiosity about when she was a baby, and oftentimes had questions I couldn't fully answer. She was eager to know more about her mom, so we'd spend a lot of time talking at night about when she was little, and what her mom was like.

With regard to child rearing tactics, there were three things I was good at: music, Spanish, and sports. I figured I would focus on teaching my kids everything I was good at and let the world dictate anything else they would need to know. I immediately enrolled the kids in piano lessons. They had a wonderful teacher who would come to the house once a week. We began speaking only Spanish in the house. I would bring the kids with me to my swim workouts and have them swim with me.

I taught them everything I could, and continue to do so. Everything else they have figured out on their own or through the help of family and friends.

The phrase I heard again and again from so many people was, "You have to be Mom *and* Dad now." I came to the conclusion that wasn't true. I could never be Mom. I could only be myself, and I was going to do whatever it took to be the father my children deserved.

I took heed to the advice of my baseball coach: "Focus on what's important and don't pay attention to what's happening in the stands." In this case the most important thing was my children, and I was going to give them everything I had.

CHAPTER 12:
JUST ADD WATER

I tried processing my grief only through music, but it was not enough. I realized that I needed something more. That "something more" I was so desperately searching for turned out to be another form of therapy I'd already tapped into right after the accident: swimming. Swimming saved my life.

I wrote this poem the same week I decided to return to swimming:

In my desire to heal
I return to water
For a break from what I feel
I return to water
My nerves are exposed, my body is frozen
My mind, heart, and spirit are broken
To water I return amidst the grief
For water is where I find relief
Relief from the wounds that sting and burn
I started in water, and had a lifetime to learn
When I need to heal
…to water I return

My dad, always the philosopher, believes in the healing powers of swimming: "I think water is one of the most magical miracle elements we have," my father surmises. "When people swim, they get into a different mode. Something happens when you become one with your surroundings. It is really magical."

However, all the public swimming pools were closed due to the pandemic. I was desperate to be in the water again, but didn't have a swimming pool to feed that desire. What I did have was a jacuzzi that measured 12 feet by 7 feet in the middle of my backyard, which was surrounded by bushes and a few trees. As I was staring at the backyard and the water, something clicked. I decided to tie an elastic band around one of the trees, then secure it around my waist. I jumped in the jacuzzi and tested the strength of the band, then started swimming in a form of controlled drowning. It's sort of like swimming in place. I needed the calm and peace that the water brought me; to be submerged, or floating, with my mind silenced.

It worked for a time, but soon it wasn't enough. When the pools opened back up in May of 2020, I never missed a day.

In the pool, it was usually me, Diego, and a couple of other people. We would swim at noon, right in the middle of the day. I would work out in the morning, then swim, and afterwards I would take a nap. In the midst of my daily routine, I would spend time with the kids and handle real life. The new routine helped me to slowly look forward to the next day. This lasted for a good part of that year.

Throughout that time, I would catch myself thinking about life before kids, and before Christina – when I was a competitive swimmer in college. When you have kids and a wife and you are working all the time, you can lose yourself in many ways. I would get remnants of who I was as an entertainer, but when COVID-19 stopped the world, there was no place to entertain, either. The water began to help me regain a sense of who I used to be – but it also provided the outlet I needed to become a better person, father, entertainer, and friend.

It was challenging to manage my old sense of competitiveness once I got in shape and started swimming more often with others. Diego said he could see it, and he could feel it.

Describing my competitive spirit, Diego says, "When Matt returned, the team I was coaching was also swimming at the same time. Matt would say, 'Diego, I just need to get in the water.' So, he would stay in his lane and go at it. But then, after one hundred yards of warming up, I noticed he was already chasing swimmers in the next lane. Matt would get immersed in his speed; his mind just switched everything else off. If the person next to him was faster, they would go at it until Matt figured out how to save himself so he could beat the next swimmer. Matt's competitive spirit is one of a champion. With a personality like that, he can turn everything else off for that hour. Matt would say 'I'm just going to go easy today, Diego, is that alright?' I would crack a sly smile knowing what really was going to happen, and reply 'Hey, whatever you want, Matt.' But that is never how the workout unfolded. Never. Matt just goes at it, full speed ahead."

My swimming routine did bring back a sense of normalcy. It was the central event of my daily life. It provided a healthy foundation upon which to ground my day. Swimming was something I did not always look forward to; it was not always easy, but I treated it like it was my job.

Slowly, swimming took me to a space where I felt like the sun had come out again. It was good to be out of the house and doing something for myself. I have always enjoyed being a part of nature and surrounded by elite athletes. At the pool, I was around like-minded people.

Swimming centered me, and then my music really started to come around. I began writing even more, and started to build the next phase of my career. Performing at the highest level is what Christina and I worked so hard toward as a unit. Other than coaching basketball, everything she had been doing was for the bands and our family. My career had to be intact in order for me to move forward and provide for my family, but my mental well-being had to come first. I needed to make sure I could still work because I love what I do. I *love* what I do. My job and my kids are my purpose. My reason for being. I had to be strong for my children, and swimming always helped me with that.

Diego notes, "Even today, as you read this, Matt's running around with the kids. He is kind of a taxi driver delivering them to events and workouts and all the stuff that the kids do. And he just cannot wait to get into the pool even if it lasts a half hour. He goes really hard at it and I think it's a way to release all that tension."

My life was coming back together, and it all went hand in hand: the water made me feel like myself again, which extended to my music. And, oddly, the most reassuring thing about swimming was the pain from physical exertion. I knew swimming was a life-long treasure, and the sport would continue to save me throughout my life.

Maintaining focus was the key. There were times I wanted to quit, but it was a task I had to complete. I swam with a group; there was social interaction. When you are training correctly you deal with mind-numbing pain that one can only experience as an endurance athlete. You dive into the pool and turn all those voices off in your head, and you just go. I was used to feeling that pain, and at least it was a pain at the time that I could identify and try to tame. I knew where it was coming from, and that I could fight through it. Losing your wife, it just hits you in so many ways. I did not know how or when the pain was going to attack me, and I sometimes had difficulty coping with it. I had to learn that, but the pain from swimming was identifiable. I have encountered it my whole life.

The results from swimming are immediate and make me feel like I'm still in the fight. However, the most important and reassuring feeling amid my own personal crisis was I could move on by swimming and the physical pain goes away with rest; it's a pain that ends, unlike the devastation of losing Christina.

Like me, the pull of the water's healing properties was too strong for Penny to resist. Penny began to play varsity water polo at Mater Dei High School, a powerhouse for sports. Penny is a great student, usually scoring straight A's. She is a stud. She works hard, and knows what it takes to be in the hunt to play. She is without a doubt one of the best swimmers on the team, and she is learning the subtleties of being a complete player.

When asked about her transition to water polo, Penny explains, "I was playing basketball, but through that, I realized how much I missed water polo. I really started to play water polo when I was fourteen. Initially I was not particularly good, but I stuck with it, and now I *know* this is my sport and I know this is what I want to do. Water polo has been the biggest grounding sport for me, just like my dad's swimming. It is my favorite thing in the world right now; it fills me up. Playing water polo in high school is like gaining a second family."

I have so much pride when I watch Penny play, but it's hard not to see that she's the spitting image of Christina. She has her mom's fire and competitive spirit. Watching her is like watching Christina.

Penny can be a little bit pensive at times, because of everything she has gone through, but she is strong as hell.

"The best way to explain it is that I know that my mother wants me to do my best," Penny states of her mom. "She's a force that I want to play for. I know what she would say, I know what drove her and I have the same drive. I tap into this mindset when I go and play. I can feel my mother playing through me."

Coincidentally, Diego is also Penny's swimming coach at Mater Dei, a job he assumed by happenstance. Penny and Diego have a wonderful relationship. He is such a positive influence. My nephew, Kaikea Roe, is the assistant coach. Penny has this wonderful "water" family surrounding her, pushing her, and being supportive.

Diego, the same person who helped me get back in the water, who helped me get my head straight, and who inspired me to continue swimming, is now doing the same for Penny. We really have a beautiful, serendipitous situation now.

"We all just need to talk to that black line sometimes," Diego reminds us.

Penny was awarded the team's "Most Improved Player" in a feature story in 2024 by the *Orange County Register*, playing on a team that made it all the way to its CIF championship game. She was also named "Most Valuable Player" at the Junior Olympics, where her team took home the gold.

On June 15, 2024, I was getting ready to play a gig on the beach in Huntington Beach, when Penny came running up to me with the biggest smile on her face, screaming, "Oh my God, oh my God, oh my God, DAD!"

"What? What is it?" I'd asked, as she stretched her arm out and shoved her phone in my face.

"Just, LOOK!" she squealed.

I looked down at her phone, and grinned ear to ear. June 15 was the first day college recruiters were allowed to contact students entering their junior year of high school to try and entice them to play for their universities. And the moment they were allowed to reach out, she got a text from University of California Santa Barbara about playing water polo for them.

"What do I say? What do I do?" she'd asked me, face filled with equal parts concern and excitement.

I replied, "This is amazing, Pen! I can't say I'm surprised, but why don't you send her a message letting her know you can talk next week."

By the end of the show, two more universities had reached out, and in the coming weeks she was contacted by UCLA, USC, Harvard, Yale, Michigan, Indiana, Cal Berkeley, Penn State, and several others. We were all over the moon for her.

In November of 2024 Penny accepted a scholarship to play Division I water polo at Indiana University in Bloomington, Indiana, where she will continue to make waves in the pool while earning her degree in Business.

CHAPTER 13:
THAT'S LIFE

It is often said that grief comes in waves. Sometimes the waves bring an overwhelming surge of emotions to the shore, only to recede after a while, leaving a silent, empty space. The waves can be triggered by a place, a smell, or even a fleeting thought, leaving you breathless and disoriented. Then, right when it feels like you've begun to breathe again, another wave hits as if the loss is fresh, reminding you that healing is not linear.

Christina and I had put an offer on a new house about two weeks before she died. I shut that down immediately after the accident. Moving to a new house would have been impossible. I had to quickly re-evaluate everything, and having my children abruptly leave behind the only home they ever knew, without their mother, would have been traumatic. We needed to stay put.

I had a sports car I loved, an Infiniti Q60. I remember when we were at the dealership, Christina said to me, "You look sexy in that car." So, I got the car. As soon as she died, I got rid of it and bought a used Lincoln Navigator, because I needed something that could get my kids from place to place. That was the focus.

I tried to manage everything Christina did to the best of my ability. *I can figure this thing out*, I'd thought to myself. What an absolute fool I was to believe that.

My son recently had to have a biopsy on a spot in his mouth, which the doctors speculated could be cancerous. I was completely rattled by it and did not get the biopsy results for 12 days. It was benign, thank God, but for 12 days I wrung my hands, running through every possible scenario. He also recently had something called "orbital cellulitis" where his eye swelled shut and he was in the hospital for four days. It is an illness he has had before, but dealing with it a second time didn't make it any easier. It is so hard to keep your kids healthy and it scares the hell out of me. It is terrifying to watch your kids go through health issues that are beyond your control.

A sick child triggers everything. It triggers the triggers. It reminds you of how vulnerable we are. Christina was vigilant about our children's health; she remembered everything and had an amazing mind for detail, which got things done. We felt safe. I just hoped to support her and keep her happy. That was my job. Christina took care of the kids' appointments and ailments, and I took care of her and supported the family however I could. Christina took care of me, too. She kept the world at bay and could tell people things I could not. I'm a big enough fish in the small pond of Orange County that people constantly want my attention.

A few weeks before Christina died, we went to a retirement party for a lifeguard we knew. Christina and I walked in, and they said, "Matt, you're here! Would you come up and sing a song?" All these people chimed in: "Would you please? Please?"

Christina stepped in and said, "He is with me tonight. This is one night I get to be with my husband. Thank you for asking, but Matt will not be performing."

I looked at my friend, the retiree, and said, "Oh, sorry, that's the law."

I did not think much about it at the time. I would have performed. Christina said, "I don't want to share you tonight."

So I said, "OK."

When I lost Christina, I suddenly did not have her as the buffer between me and everything else. And I did not realize how important that buffer was. I did when it was gone. But life does not stop, and we have had to come to grips with that.

I still do an occasional interview, using the media attention to raise awareness for the Christina Mauser Foundation – something we created in her honor, soon after she passed. The foundation supports women and girls in sports through scholarships. Christina was a fierce, talented, and competitive high school athlete with incredible empathy and a tenacious spirit. The foundation's goal is to offer scholarships to senior high school student-athletes who exemplify the same qualities as Christina, not only to assist those in need, but to ensure Christina's name and legacy live on forever. As of the publishing date of this book, the foundation has awarded more than $100,000 in scholarships.

Though I hope to keep the life and legacy of my wife alive through the foundation, I know that she also lives on through our children. My daughter, Ivy, wants to see videos of her mom all the time and I will let her watch, but it destroys me. Videos bring back every memory, and after watching them I'm emotionally drained for a couple of days. From time to time my mind forgets, but video footage of my wife brings the pain to the present. It is so clear, so real.

August 23 is Kobe's birthday, and the public celebrates August 24 (8/24, for Kobe's two jersey numbers with the Lakers) as Kobe Day. Three years after the helicopter crash, they announced on Kobe Day that the Lakers would unveil a new statue of Kobe on 8/24/2024. I see public worship of Kobe, and I think, *My wife died on that same helicopter.*

Penny had her own realization, at the Happiest Place on Earth, of all places: "I went to Disneyland recently and saw many people wearing Mamba sweatshirts," Penny frustratingly recalls. "I read an article which discussed Kobe, Gianna, *and seven others*, which is upsetting to me because one of those 'others' was my mom."

I see Christina in all my children. I see Penny playing for her water polo team, determined to keep getting better.

I see Ivy lighting up the room when she comes on stage at my concerts.

I see Tom growing, playing music, and finding his own way. I remember when Tom was little, Kobe used to say, "Look how long that kid's arms are!"

In 2023, Tom decided to give up water polo for basketball. Basketball is a much harder road to earn scholarships for college. Southern California is a water polo hotbed and there are many opportunities because coaches come from all over the country to find talent here. Every state has basketball players. He's 6-foot-3 at age 14 and is developing quickly as a player.

He's currently being recruited by private high schools, but it will be a considerable amount of work to stand out in such a competitive sport. So, I asked Tom why he wanted to take the more difficult path.

Tom looked me dead in the eyes and said, "Because Mom played basketball, and I want to do it, too."

CHAPTER 14:
MY TWO MEXICAN WIVES

In the middle of the emotional shitstorm we were in, two remarkable women with unwavering support and love became pillars of strength and comfort when we needed it most. It has been through our nannies, Alma and Betty, that I have learned raising three young children who have suffered such a catastrophic loss may not be easy, but through patience and understanding (and a whole lot of help), it *is* possible.

Alma had been Ivy's part-time nanny for a couple of years while Christina and I were still teaching. When Christina died, Alma and her good friend Betty came to me and said, "You're going to need help. Here's what we think: we are going to come every morning, and we are going to leave at night. We will be here every day, except for Sunday. We will split the days." A rushing sense of sadness washed over me with the realization that the kids were not going to be raised by their mother and I. It was heartbreaking. For a while I felt sorry for myself and my kids. I was almost resentful that I had to resort to a nanny for their basic and maternal needs. But little by little, as we began to heal, I looked at them both as my allies and a big part of my village. They have dedicated their lives to helping me raise my three children, especially Ivy who was three when she lost her mom. My heart softened and they became family. They immediately jumped in, helping me care for the children while also feeding us, keeping the house in order, and helping me manage the daily influx of information and complexities that come with the territory of being a recent widower. It took about a year before I could see Alma and Betty and not associate them with the loss of Christina.

Having two nannies was a financial strain, but it was worth

every penny; my children loved them, and it helped give them a sense of normalcy, of stability, of love. What price tag would you put on your children's well-being?

Alma went to nursing school in Mexico and had been a nurse in Acapulco. She has been a nanny for more than 30 years. Alma's quick wit and humor have been a welcome addition to the family, but it's her calm, soothing demeanor that I appreciate most. She is such an important voice for me. When I would start to spiral, get upset or lose control of my emotions, Alma would say in her sweet voice, "Calm down, relax, relax." In the midst of chaos, she has always had the innate ability to diffuse any situation, offering a quiet kind of empathy and forbearance.

Betty has been a nanny for more than 20 years. When her mother passed away she was 19 years old, and her youngest sister was only nine. Betty was the middle child of 13, and the experience of raising her younger siblings has given her a unique perspective on helping me care for children who have suffered the loss of their mother.

I was extremely fortunate to have their steadying hands and familiar faces to guide me. The kids did not have their mom, but they had mother figures who helped cook for them, braid the girls' hair, and get them ready in the morning. These women were not trying to replace my children's mother in any way, shape, or form – they were almost like an extension of her; a way for my kids to have a loving female presence consistently in their lives.

Alma and Betty have always been in constant communication with one another about what was going on with the kids, and were deep in the trenches with us. Family and friends would check in on us, and sometimes the kids would have an attitude or give them flak. Alma and Betty would help the kids process their feelings in a very caring and compassionate way, ensuring they knew that they weren't alone.

They'd take the kids outside to play, just to get them out of the house. They'd talk with them, cry with them, and help them understand that they had to keep going because life doesn't just stop once someone dies. "It's the hardest thing to have to live through, but we have to find the light to help us keep going," Betty explains.

It was really difficult for Tom to open up right after Christina died, but when Alma or Betty would talk to him one-on-one, he would have a lot of questions about why and how something like this could happen. Alma spoke with him about God and faith in ways that would reassure him and give him peace. Initially, Tom would get very defensive and upset when Alma or Betty would tell him to clean his room or do his chores. He would shut down and tune everyone out. Eventually he began to listen, and they helped turn him into such a responsible young man.

When it finally clicked with Ivy that Mom really wasn't coming home, she had so many questions about where her mom went and why. Alma was there to gently guide her through the healing process with God. "I would tell Ivy, 'You can pray to God when you are feeling angry or sad about your mother or anything else,'" Alma remembers. "You can pray that your mother comes to visit you in your dreams, and that she will watch over and protect you.'"

Christina had a strong sense of faith, and I'm so grateful that Alma has been very vocal about God with the kids. They've all been in private schools the past several years, furthering their education about religion as well. I know it's what Christina would have wanted.

Betty's daughter, Valentina, is Ivy's age and the two have become thick as thieves. It has been wonderful to watch the evolution of their friendship and see how strong their bond is. They can give each other a simple look and know exactly what the other is thinking. Sometimes they're a bit mischievous, but having that kind of friendship with someone is rare. They talk about their futures, their dreams, and what they're going to do together when they get older. Betty and Alma will joke with the girls that since they used to push them in a stroller when they were younger, when Betty and Alma are older, the girls will have to push them around in wheelchairs and be the ones to take care of them.

"Matt always makes us feel like we're part of the family," Betty adds. "He always treats us with respect and usually introduces us as his 'Mexican wives,' which we think is so funny. We know he cares about us and appreciates how important a role we play in the kids' lives. I had a family emergency back in 2021 and couldn't work for about a month. Matt stepped in and sent me money to help with bills while I was out, and I will never forget his kindness or generosity."

When the extended family members wanted to take the kids out, Alma would be the go-between when I wasn't around. "Other people think that they can override Matt's decisions as a father, but they don't when we are around. If Matt doesn't want the kids to do something, we respect his wishes," Alma maintains.

As serious as the situations were that we've gone through together, there have been many lighthearted moments between us. For instance, their favorite singer isn't me – it's Luis Miguel, and they *always* remind me of it. They send me video clips of him for "inspiration," and make fun of my dancing. They're always quick to have a good laugh at my expense, and I love it.

"Even through all the dark times there were many good memories we created with Matt and the kids, and still do," notes Betty. "We have experiences like going to Disneyland, dinners, vacations, and creating new traditions. During Christmas we do Secret Santa gifts with them, and go to the boat parade in Newport Beach. It's something that the kids look forward to every year."

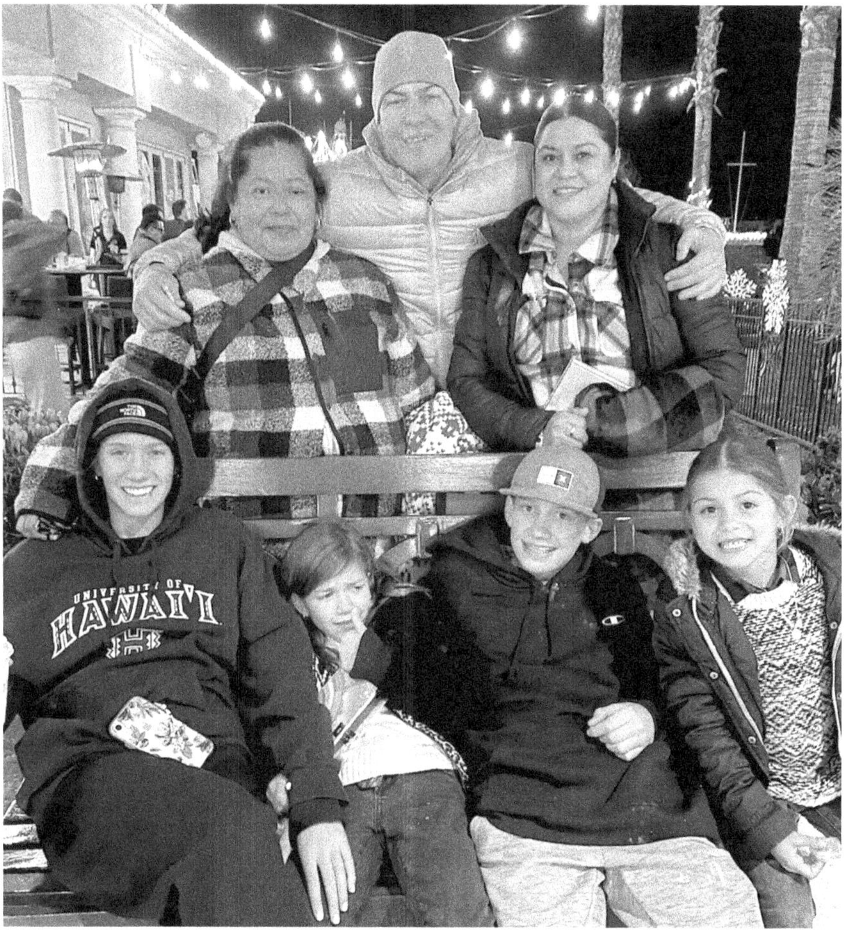
UNIVERSITY OF
HAWAI'I

CMAC

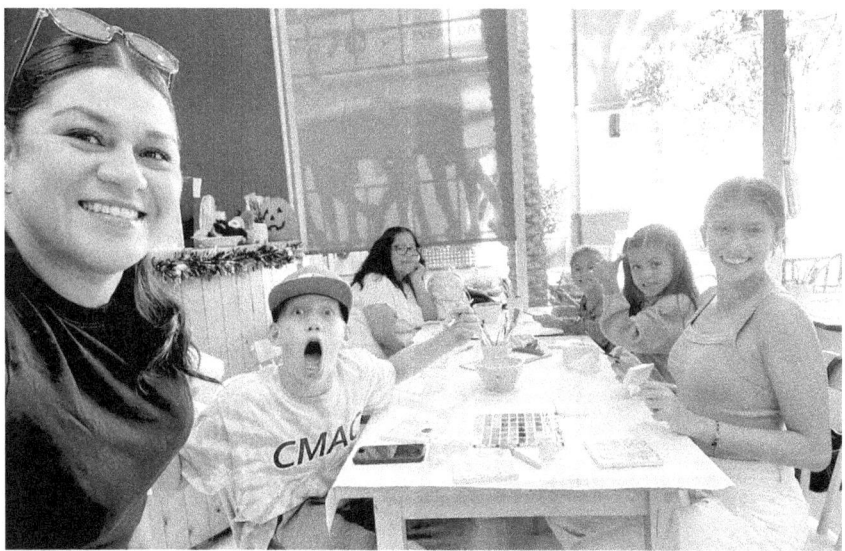

Penny sums up her relationship with them like this: "I love Alma and Betty. They will not hesitate to let Dad know that he's out of line sometimes. Aside from Dad, Betty and Alma are our biggest supporters and I know that they carried a lot of heavy weight that sometimes we couldn't handle. And they knew that we needed them. They held this huge burden for us and kept us going. Even through COVID they stuck with us. When we got them sick, they still came and said, 'We love you guys, and we're here for you.' They help with everything around the house. Additionally, I've cried to Alma and Betty and I've confided in them some of my biggest secrets. I trust them completely."

When I got to a point where I thought I'd be able to start dating again, Betty and Alma became the gatekeepers of my social life. I couldn't get past the first date with someone without them stepping in and giving me their two cents. It was usually a stern look or a shake of the finger. If Alma doesn't like you, you'll know it. She is very protective of the kids and anyone who enters their lives.

In an early interview with Anderson Cooper right after Christina passed, he said something that really resonated with me over the last several years. He said that you'll find people who will help you through your grief who you never expected to be there for you. They will understand and be able to help you navigate your new "normal." You have to be open to receiving their kindness but you have to be aware and able to recognize when good people come into your life. Then there will be people you always thought would be there for you, and weren't. And that's OK.

Alma and Betty were two of those unexpected heroes who I'm so glad I recognized. I knew I needed help with the kids, but could never have imagined the lengths to which they would go to care for my children. I hope that one day I am able to do something very special for them to show how much I appreciate everything they have done for my family.

CHAPTER 15:
THE REAL TREASURE

When I made the decision to go on *America's Got Talent*, the purpose was to be an example of resilience for my kids, to keep their mother's memory alive, and raise awareness for The Christina Mauser Foundation. I like to think I was able to accomplish those things by putting myself out there and allowing myself to be vulnerable. It was not an easy thing to do, but it was worth it.

Now, music truly is a family affair. All three kids are still taking piano lessons, and Tom has been learning how to play the bass guitar and drums as well. Some of my favorite days are spent goofing around and singing with them while one of us plays the piano or guitar. Since Tom and Penny were little, they've always come up on stage during performances at different concerts to dance and/or sing along with me. Nowadays, I turn them loose whenever they accompany me to a Tijuana Dogs show and watch in amazement as Penny belts out "Rock and Roll" by Led Zeppelin or "Party in the U.S.A." by Miley Cyrus, and Tom crushes "Uptown Funk" by Bruno Mars or "Song 2" by Blur.

More and more songs are being added to their repertoire, and they always bring the house down. Penny and I do a duet to "Something Stupid" by Frank and Nancy Sinatra during my Sinatra-style big band shows, then she'll tear up the stage on her own with "These Boots Are Made for Walkin'," by Nancy Sinatra.

Something
Stupid

These Boots are
Made for Walkin'

Ivy made her debut on stage singing, "These Boots are Made for Walkin'," with Penny during a sold out show in December of 2023 and she knocked it out of the park. She was seven years old.

Since then, she's constantly been up on stage with me at Tijuana Dogs shows singing and dancing to an original song I wrote (Ivy and Valentina starred in the music video for it, so she has a certain fondness for the song), called "CHP." She has also stepped into big sister Penny's shoes by performing the song that kept Penny off the helicopter on that fateful day, "Green Bike," with me during a few concerts when Penny was unable to perform.

CHP

The growth in popularity of both The Matt Mauser Big Band (formerly The Sinatra Big Band) and Tijuana Dogs has made a massive and positive impact on my life, which in turn has profoundly affected the lives of my children as well.

They love being a part of it. The most important thing to me, and the only thing that really matters at the end of the day, is that my kids are happy and becoming successful, kind human beings. My job is to help my kids be the absolute best version of themselves they can be. Everything else is insignificant. My kids are trying to live their best life, despite the loss they had to endure. They are thriving, they're happy, they have friends, and to me, that is so crucial to their development. My joy is in watching them pursue their dreams.

Ivy makes loom bracelets and friendship bracelets to sell during my shows, while Tom and Penny sell t-shirts, hats, and other merchandise.

My children are getting a firsthand understanding of business dynamics, teaching them valuable lessons in customer service, inventory management, and sales. Together, they are discovering the many facets of the music business and have eagerly assumed many of the duties that Christina used to help me with. In the summer of 2024, Tijuana Dogs played a local concert series, drawing record crowds. Penny and Tom managed the merchandise table, selling shirts and hats, while Ivy sold her bracelets. They would join me on the stage, sing a song, and then return to the side and start selling. Penny and Tom are compensated a percentage of everything they sell (a large portion of the proceeds from shirt sales goes toward benefitting The Christina Mauser Foundation), and that is how they pay for what they want to do.

Though my children have become extremely comfortable on

stage, they do not actively seek the spotlight on a larger scale. Recently, we received an offer to be part of a reality television show about raising kids as a single parent. One of the producers follows my social media accounts and mentioned that he saw most of my posts of the kids performing on stage and doing other day-to-day activities, such as dance routines, playing basketball, or going to the beach; just the normal kind of things dads do with their kids. He loved the togetherness of our family.

The proposal seemed a little bit sensationalized, but it was going to be based on our everyday life and how our family was living through the loss of a parent/significant other. I considered the offer for about a day before running the idea past the kids. In a united front, they said, "Hell, no. We do not want that." And just like that, I told the producers we would have to pass. I was on the fence about it, but if the kids weren't 100% on board, there was no way I was going to make them do anything they weren't comfortable doing.

My job as a performer has taken me to some incredible places. I've played on top of the World Trade Center, and performed at Mar-A-Lago at five separate New Year's Eve celebrations for President Donald Trump. I sang at Tiffany Trump's wedding, and we're booked for many major corporate gigs.

I still work with David Foster, who is a consummate professional and extremely humble. David made Michael Bublé a star after seeing him sing at a wedding. He co-wrote "I Have Nothing" for Whitney Houston. He has a show called "Hitman: David Foster and Friends," where he rotates through top-of-the-line singers like Andrea Bocelli, Katharine McPhee, Pia Toscano, and Loren Allred (who sang "Never Enough" in *The Greatest Showman*), to mention a few. And now, I am in that rotation. Performing with such a renowned musician and composer is an electrifying experience for which I am forever grateful.

It is still very much a balancing act to try and maintain focus when my mind starts to wander into dark places. After the adrenaline rush of performing shows on the weekend, it's often hard to wind down. Mondays are especially challenging because that's when the energy from performing or going from game to game, supporting my kids in their different sports and activities, begins to fade. When Christina was alive, if things were getting hectic we would always sit on the front porch, and she'd say, "Let's have a beer." We weren't big drinkers, but the simple comfort of each other's company was a great way to connect and relax. I attempted to do that the other day, but it wasn't the same without her beside me – there was no laughter to fill the quiet, no gentle conversation to relax my mind. Flashbacks like that remain the hardest to bear. And even the most mundane tasks bring memories of her to the foreground. When I tuck my kids in, Tom will hug a picture of him and his mom. He holds the picture next to his heart, and it just fractures mine.

One of the most interesting things that happened amid the immense loss is that my dad returned to my life. It was like having a missing puzzle piece return, and we are both learning how to fit together again. Having him here, in this new chapter, has added layers to a deepening relationship I never expected to have.

"Every time we talked for a year and a half, or maybe two years,

I listened and let Matt unload," my dad remembers. "There were not too many people who were there with him during that process. Many could not see what he was going through. When he walks out his door, he turns into the performer. I got in my car the minute I heard about Christina, and I told my wife I was going. I got a bed, put it on the floor, and lived in Matt's garage for three weeks. I did not want him to go through this alone. I needed to make up for the fact that I deserted Matt when he was a little boy. I said, 'Here's your chance, George.' This was 2020, and I was 78 years old. I know he was not a kid anymore, but I am glad I made that decision to be with him. Matt was deeply, deeply wounded. It has been a blessing to be back in Matt's life. Now I speak with him every few days because we are karmically connected. I do not know what it is, but we're a lot alike in some ways."

They say that with the passage of time things will get better. And for the most part, they do. There is a level of improvement, a healing that takes place, where the unrelenting ache from deep inside your chest isn't as significant. But it never goes away.

I was unable to replicate our day-to-day life and handle the band responsibilities on my own. I hired an assistant, a booking agent, and an overall manager for my music career – in addition to having the nannies, Christina's family, and a social media manager. It takes all these people just to fill the void she left in our daily lives, let alone the one in our hearts. However, creating a stable environment for my kids has always come first – it's the most important thing I feel I can do.

Six mornings a week, either Alma or Betty shows up around 9 a.m. I usually go to the gym, and then I will take the kids, especially in the summertime, to their activities. I manage the home business, make phone calls, and try to get all the business concerning my bands squared away before I spend the day taking care of kids, carpooling, or whatever I need to do. I try to swim at night, before I hit the stage for my shows. Our life has reached a respectful cadence. We get pedicures together as a family, go on day trips to the beach or Disneyland, or we play games around the house. We recently got a weight set in the garage, so we have been working out together, keeping everybody healthy. With Alma and Betty, we have become a family unit and we are working hard to raise these kids. We keep them busy, and they keep us busy. Christina's family also plays a big role in the kids' lives, and their support is a lifeline that brings stability and familiarity.

When we finally moved out of our house in 2022, I purchased all new beds and made sure the new house was fully decorated. I did not move any of our old furniture. I can never recreate what we had while Christina was with us, so I wanted a clean, fresh start for all of us. We've kept the old house as a rental, and someday I hope one of the kids will be able to start their own family in it. The day we left our home and decided we were going to spend the night in the new house, we locked the door behind us and cried. A part of me felt I was leaving pieces of Christina and our life behind, and in a way, I was – though it was a part I knew I needed to let go. We had remained in our old house for two and a half years after Christina died. Every time I had to go back to that house to get mail or something, I'd think, *Where did my life go? What happened to everything I believed in?* The harshness of reality can be so painful.

I try to take the good with the bad as graciously as possible (it doesn't always work out that way), and I also try to give myself a break every once in a while to acknowledge the fact that I'm not perfect, nor will I ever be. I'll always be a work in progress, doing my damndest to ensure the lives of my children are full and happy.

The most important thing that I want people to know is that through the pain, we are enduring. Tom asked me the other night what my greatest accomplishment was. It was an easy answer: meeting his mom, and then surviving through her loss to raise our children to be the people that they are becoming.

His question took me back to a formative time in my life. As a lifeguard, you spend the majority of your job being proactive, not reactionary, like many other agencies. When you see somebody who can't swim, is swimming in a dangerous area, or is stuck in a rip current being sucked out to sea, you step into action, either preventing them from these dangers or helping them once they're in those situations.

Being proactive in rescuing people is something I've carried with me throughout my life. It is the same principle behind searching for joy and finding the treasures in life after grief overtakes you. When something so crushing shatters your life, there can be a complacency in letting life fall where it may and just reacting to whatever is thrown at you. I've had to consciously make the decision to be proactive in my life and search for everyday treasures. That is why I call this book *Bittersweet Treasures,* because there are treasures out there – but sometimes you have to really dig and work hard to find them. And once you find them, it's bittersweet because you can't share them with the person you've lost. Things we identified as treasures in our youth, such as earning money or prestige, notoriety, or fame, had meant so much at the time. But, as life goes on, the little treasures you find along the way can become much more significant than you ever imagined possible. Fond memories, learning, growing, always striving to be the absolute best version of yourself – those are treasures no one can ever take from you.

A big step in healing from such a catastrophic personal loss is understanding what makes you happy. Understanding that it's possible to even *be* happy again. You must pursue every avenue or lead you come across that could potentially light the way toward a brighter future. Keep putting one foot in front of the other, because in time you won't just be walking in circles – you'll be forging a path of your own that will be worth the fight.

Nostalgia has been painfully bittersweet, especially when I find myself relating everything to losing Christina. But even in its ache, nostalgia has brought me clarity. I see the undeniable ways I've influenced my son to grow into a young man, and my daughters into young ladies. I've witnessed my son hold doors open for his sisters, showing respect and kindness. I've seen him treat elders with dignity and grace. I've watched my daughter, Penny, articulate her thoughts with such poise and meaning during a reporter's interview. I've seen her endure fierce battles in water polo, winning and losing with humility and fire in equal measure.

All of this grace, strength, and character comes from the simple, intentional act of keeping life uncomplicated and pouring my energy into my children after tragedy struck. And now, I'm beginning to see the payoff. My treasure isn't buried on a distant beach, nor does it await in some grand payday. No, my hidden treasure – my bittersweet treasure – is here. It's watching my children navigate life with resilience, finding their way in a world that was shaken when they lost the most important person in it.

For being their anchor, I've filled a void that haunted me for so much of my own life. And maybe, just maybe, living the first part of my life without a father, searching for new heroes, and learning the hard lessons on my own was part of a larger plan. Because now, standing here and connecting the dots, it's all starting to make sense.

THE LAST KISS – A LOVE LETTER

My Dearest Christina,

On the morning we lost you, the last connection we ever had was a kiss. You kissed my lips and said, "I love you." I was half asleep, and when I finally responded, the door was being closed and you walked out to go to work. That kiss has both haunted and sustained me. Your final show of affection will last me a lifetime. A lifetime dedicated to you and the beautiful children we created and nurtured. That kiss was all I needed, my sweet wife and best friend. That kiss was the last kiss of thousands of wonderful kisses that strengthened our bond, and was enough to help me endure an agonizing 2020 full of loss and uncertainty.

Your kiss was enough to encourage me to go back to work and find my music and voice again. Your kiss was enough to take the kids to school and practices, to doctor appointments and family functions. Your kiss got me through all the painful anniversaries, birthdays, and holidays. Your kiss was enough.

But there will come a day, my dear, that the kiss will have to just be an eternal sign of our love. For love, like life, must be experienced daily. My wound is deep and wide, but it is healing and continues to heal. At some point, I have to let you go. I will keep the memory of the kiss, but allow your light to shine without occupying such a painful place in my heart.

So I'll say goodbye for now, and if God or whatever beautiful ending brings us together again, I will return that beautiful kiss and hold you in my arms for eternity.

I love you, Christina. I always have, and I always will.

Forever yours, Your husband, Matt

EPILOGUE

It has been five years since I last saw Christina's smile light up a room and watched as she owned a dance floor. My heart still aches, and my head still swims with memories of our life together, but I move forward holding the hands of our children while living my life in a way that would hopefully make her proud. I pray that our kids always remember the warrior their mom was, and how fiercely she loved them.

Being married to Christina, then losing her, really illustrated how important happiness was to me. Nothing is going to replace her. No success, money, or career is ever going to change the reality of losing my wife. I've had to learn how to appreciate life and all its imperfections. In order to do that, I needed to stay active and engaged in the day-to-days. But inwardly, during moments of silence and reflection, I have had to be honest with myself and let go of my expectations of what life holds for me. I'm still in the process of learning to enjoy life as it comes.

I've always taken pride in my work as a performer, but now when I see the look of pure joy on the faces in the crowd while they dance and sing along with me, it brings a new kind of fulfillment to my life. Making others happy makes *me* happy. When I tell my story, or sing a certain song, I connect with the audience in a way that transcends the grief I have lived with. There are moments when I feel like I'm really touching people's hearts. There's a part of me that feels that maybe I'm here to tell my story, and to help others move through grief in a meaningful way. As painful as the last five years have been, if anything good can come of it, I'll take it.

May 6, 2025, would have marked 20 years since we said "'Til death do us part." Christina may have passed on, but she will *always* be a part of me. I see her every day in our children, and in the kindness of others. I still see the positive impact she made in the lives of so many, and it warms my heart. To know Christina was to love her, and man, did I ever. More than anything, I am humbled by the way she loved me.

I heard somewhere that life is for the living. Nothing could be closer to the truth. I am finally at a point in my grief where I'm ready to take on the next chapter and be open to whatever the future may hold. Life is precious, and I want to be present in every moment. It's not always doable, but I will sure as hell try.

For more information about The Christina Mauser Foundation, please visit www.christinamauserfoundation.org.

The Christina Mauser Foundation

ACKNOWLEDGEMENTS

With love and gratitude:

Penny, Tom, and Ivy, there are literally no words to accurately describe the depth of my love for you. You are the center of my universe, my entire reason for being, and I hope you know that I am *forever* in your corner. I know in my soul that your mother is so very proud of each one of you, and that she will never stop watching over you. Always trust yourself, make good decisions, and surround yourself with kind and compassionate people.

Alma and Betty, you are more than our nannies — you are earth angels who will always be a part of our family. The loving ways in which you have helped me raise the children in Christina's absence are endless. Having mother figures like the two of you in their lives has been such a gift. Thank you for all you have done, and continue to do, for our family.

Katie Brandenburger, you are not just my social media manager — you are the one who does all the little things that nobody else can do. Without you, this book wouldn't have been possible.

Cheri Westly, you are an extraordinary person of many talents. Your ability to multitask and maintain our hectic schedules while simultaneously ensuring our lives are in sync is mind-blowing. You are a true blessing in our lives.

Bernadette Tran, you are my rock and give so much of yourself everyday. It doesn't go unnoticed. **Logan and Luka**, you always make me laugh and give the best hugs.

Christina's family, whoever said "it takes a village" to raise children hit the nail on the head. You have surrounded us with a strong, loving, and tight knit village that consistently makes my children feel loved. From carpooling to throwing birthday parties and all the little things in between, you are appreciated more than you know.

My family, you were there for me when I needed you most. **Dad,** the late-night conversations, words of encouragement, and advice are exactly what I've needed. My step-mother, **Gail,** thank you for always showing your support in everything I do. **Mom,** stepping up with the kids has been so helpful.

John McEntee and Thomas Kinmartin, you are my voices of reason and keep the bands working. You also stepped in when I needed you most.

Tijuana Dogs and The Matt Mauser Big Band musicians, you help make it all work — especially my brother in musicality, **Dave Murdy,** who opened the door that led me into the world of music.

Pete Jacobs, you have believed in me and shared your musical genius.

Darren Vegas and Steve Denenberg, you encouraged me to get back into the studio and continue writing music during my darkest hour. You were right — it helped.

Mike Cassity, thanks for listening, buddy.

Diego Pombo, you got me back in the water and helped bring me back to life.

My water polo, swimming, and lifeguard families, I cherish the brotherhood you have made me a part of.

The Christina Mauser Foundation team, you play such a huge role in keeping Christina's memory alive.

Tijuana Dogs and The Matt Mauser Big Band fans, you consistently show up and have always been there for us in so many ways. Thank you.

• • • • •

To Michael Brandenburger, Cheri and Perry Westly, Dennis and Diane Marchand, and Michele L.: You made the impossible possible, and have saved my life many times over. You are miracle workers through and through. With every ounce of my being, I thank you for your love and support. – Katie

ABOUT THE AUTHOR

Matt Mauser is a songwriter, solo artist, pop/rock bandleader for the popular Orange County-based cover band, Tijuana Dogs, and frontman for a Sinatra-style big band, who has spent more than three decades onstage and in the writing room. A lifelong resident of Southern California, he was a middle school Spanish teacher and Huntington Beach lifeguard for more than 20 years before making the leap to full-time entertainer in 2018. Matt is an *America's Got Talent* finalist, who performs regularly with 16-time GRAMMY Award winner, David Foster.

Matt is a widower and father of three incredible kids, whose ambitious sports, school, and extracurricular activities always keep him on the go. When he's not on stage, in the writing room, or spending time with his children, you can find Matt swimming laps in the pool. He currently resides in Orange County, California.

To learn more about Matt, visit www.mattmauser.com.

mattmauser.com

www.ingramcontent.com/pod-product-compliance
Lightning Source LLC
Chambersburg PA
CBHW071715140626
46557CB00011B/317